There's More to Life than Sex *&* Money

103 inspirational stories to give your life new meaning

Written and compiled by
SUE CALWELL
AND
DANIEL JOHNSON

Penguin Books

Penguin Books Australia Ltd
487 Maroondah Highway, PO Box 257
Ringwood, Victoria 3134, Australia
Penguin Books Ltd
Harmondsworth, Middlesex, England
Penguin Putnam Inc.
375 Hudson Street, New York, New York 10014, USA
Penguin Books Canada Limited
10 Alcorn Avenue, Toronto, Ontario, Canada M4V 3B2
Penguin Books (NZ) Ltd
Cnr Rosedale and Airborne Roads, Albany, Auckland, New Zealand
Penguin Books (South Africa) (Pty) Ltd
4 Pallinghurst Road, Parktown 2193, South Africa

First published by Penguin Books Australia Ltd 1997

5 7 9 10 8 6

Text design by Ellie Exarchos, Penguin Design Studio
Cover design by Sandy Cull, Penguin Design Studio
Text illustrations by Michelle Ryan
Typeset in 11/19pt Weiss by Post Pre-press Group, Brisbane
Made and printed in Australia by Australian Print Group, Maryborough, Victoria

National Library of Australia
Cataloguing-in-Publication data:

There's more to life than sex and money.

ISBN 0 14 026359 4.

1. Life change events – Psychological aspects – Case studies. 2. Courage – Case studies. I.
Calwell, Sue. II. Johnson, Daniel, 1956– .

158

The passage on pages 86–7 from *The Dutch in Australia* by
Dr Edward Duyker 1987 is reproduced by kind permission of the author.

It's true.

There's more to life than sex and money.

This book is for you if:
- You want more out of your life.
- You need a boost and want to be inspired.
- You know happiness and joy are your aim.

Sounds like some sort of advertising gimmick, doesn't it? It's not.

We've learnt a lot in life. Our friends have learnt a lot. You have learnt a lot.

This book is filled with messages everyone needs, but maybe you haven't experienced them or you haven't taken the time to learn.

Each story illustrates a powerful message. In the Action Planner at the end of each chapter, we show you how to turn these messages into positive improvements in your life.

Make the decision to change your life, now!

Sweet music to an old musician's ears. I knew I was out of rhythm.

Athol Guy, musician, The Seekers

This book is for those who feel the light at the end of the tunnel is an express train coming towards them.

Claude Lombard, LOMBARD The Paper People

This book is so honest, so truthful, so worthwhile.

Adele Palmer, fashion and homeware designer

I love this book. It is a priceless collection of life's most important messages illustrated with powerful stories. I found the Action Planner gives the reader the help they need to change their life forever for the better.

Jeanne Pratt, Pratt Industries and a philanthropist

This book is a great gift for anyone who hasn't smelled the roses lately.

Felicity Kennett, television presenter

Read this book now and then read it again in a couple of months. You'll just keep learning and improving.

David Marriner, Chairman, Marriner Theatres

We dedicate this book with all our love to you,
the readers, the people this book was written for.

There are seven young readers who are
especially important to us, our children:
Georgina, Victoria and Daniel; Yvonne, Jarvis, Paris and Yasmin.

CONTENTS

CONTENTS

CONTENTS

CONTENTS

ACKNOWLEDGEMENTS

The book you are reading is the result of input from hundreds of people. We are grateful to every single person who has supported and assisted us.

There are several people who have been especially helpful whom we wish to acknowledge:

Di Lang, who has been devoted to this project from the moment it was destined to become a book. Di gave so much time and provided us with much-needed support and advice. Her creative input and commitment has influenced this book from cover to cover.

To all our friends who provided material. Without your contributions this book would not have become a reality. We wish we could have included every single piece sent to us. It just was not possible, yet we are very appreciative of everyone's input and willingness to help.

A very special thanks to Kate Johnson and Alistair Trimble, our 'Better Halves', who have been 100 per cent supportive and given us both unlimited amounts of encouragement throughout this entire project.

Elizabeth Boydell, who contributed out of friendship and love countless hours of typing and logistical support. A very special thank you.

Maria Prendergast for believing in our concept and for introducing us to our fantastic publishers.

To everyone at Penguin Books Australia who was committed from our very first meeting to ensure this book reached as many people as possible. Particularly: Bob Sessions for his vision; Julie Gibbs for her 110 per cent commitment and belief; Michelle

Proctor and Alex Watts for their dedication; Gabrielle Coyne for her creative marketing; and Peter Blake and his team for getting out there and telling people it's true that *There's More to Life than Sex and Money*.

Miriam Cannell, our editor. We never realised how important an editor is until we met Miriam. This quote, from one of the dozens of multi-page faxes we received from Miriam, sums up her input: 'I hope I haven't gone overboard with all my queries, it's just that I want your book to be the best it can possibly be.' It is the best thanks to Miriam.

INTRODUCTION

Maybe we are slow learners but it took both of us a long time to learn that sex and money are minor not major elements in our lives. This book is about the messages life teaches us (or is trying to teach us).

We'd like you to know the book you are holding is beautiful because it is the result of one great friendship. No, actually it is the essence of many close friendships. Let us explain.

We met, as many people do, through our children. Eve (Daniel's daughter) and Georgina (Sue's daughter) became 'absolute best friends' from the moment they met as three-year-olds in kindergarten. We never realised then how much we would have to go through, how much we would support each other, or that we'd end up compiling this book together years later.

We have both been through plenty of tough times and joyous times. Daniel's children stayed with Sue the night after their mother, Daniel's wife, passed away. Sue's children stayed with Daniel when Sue was coping with some of the most difficult times the corporate world could throw at a Chief Executive. These are just two examples of when we've been there for each other no matter what.

Thank goodness we've had the desire and we made the time to talk and learn from our experiences. We have spent hundreds, possibly thousands, of hours sharing the powerful messages life has taught us.

One wet, cold and wintry Melbourne night we were sitting by the fire at Sue's house having one of our long conversations. This was one of those rare moments of insight which all too quickly seem to get lost in the frantic demands of everyday life. We both knew the messages we were discovering together were far too important to let slip by. We wanted to capture them for our families and friends, most especially for our children.

This commitment to each other has become *There's More to Life than Sex and Money*, an all-consuming passion for both of us.

Since we decided to record our most meaningful experiences, and those of our friends, nearly two years ago, we haven't stopped learning from each other and our friends. What started out as a simple three-week project of our own has turned into a major publishing commitment with Penguin. Once we started, we realised we should look beyond our immediate loved ones and strive to make a difference to as many people's lives as possible. And that's exactly what's happening with *There's More to Life than Sex and Money*.

At the start of each chapter you will find highlighted passages. These gems of wisdom come from a writing known as *Desiderata*, which has stood the test of time. We have been told it was found in the old Saint Paul's church, Baltimore, USA, dated 1692. We have reproduced *Desiderata* in its entirety for you on pages *xviii–xix*. It acts as a summary of many of the messages in this book.

In collecting these stories we have been fortunate enough to internalise many of the messages. As a result, our own lives have changed so much for the better. We want exactly the same for you.

Love life.

Daniel Johnson   Sue Calwell
Colorado, USA   Melbourne, Australia

HOW TO ENJOY THIS BOOK

This is a powerful book. Each story could have a profound impact on your life. As you read, there is no need to rush or look ahead to see how many pages are left. In fact, you are best not to read from cover to cover. Select the chapter that most appeals to you. Enjoy that first.

As you read through these stories, imagine you are hearing them from a close friend. Talk about them. Discuss the messages with friends and loved ones. What does each story tell you? Become involved, and share these stories with others.

You might choose to read or reread a story a day, a week, a month. Spread them out. Give yourself time to absorb them, enjoy them and learn from them. For example, you may choose to read a story before writing in your personal diary each day. These stories are certain to stir all sorts of emotions. You may laugh, you may cry, you may be left wondering why. Each story is personal; many you will connect with, some you may not. Don't judge them, just accept them.

To improve your life as a result of these stories requires action beyond reading. We have provided suggested actions you can take at the end of each chapter. We know these actions work wonders, and we encourage you to take positive action in your life!

TAKING ACTION TO MAKE A
DIFFERENCE IN YOUR LIFE

At the end of each chapter you will find a section titled 'Taking Action', which provides you with recommended actions you can take. These actions provide a link between the stories and the messages in this book and the positive improvements you can make in your own life.

We have learnt a tremendous amount through writing and compiling this book. Our suggestions come from our own experiences and from those of the contributors. We know they work.

You may end up taking one action or a hundred actions as a result of this book. It's not the quantity of actions but the constructive improvements that are important.

Here is an outline of the six steps we recommend you take:

STEP ONE Review each of the messages in the chapter by just scanning back through the stories. If you need to have a message illustrated again, reread the story.

STEP TWO Read through the suggested actions in the 'Taking Action' section at the end of the chapter. Place an asterisk next to each of the actions you feel strongly about. These should be the sorts of actions you really want to internalise so they become a part of your life. This step is extremely important – only highlight those actions you will implement.

STEP THREE If it seems appropriate and suits your style, number your actions in a priority sequence with number 1 being the most important. You can apply this idea to a chapter with several actions, or to all your actions from throughout the book.

STEP FOUR Customise the actions to suit you. Very few, if any, of the actions will be exactly right for you. In the space provided below your selected action/s, write what is specific to you. For example, if the action is to volunteer time to a charity or non-profit organisation, write down which one, when you will start, and how much time each week you will volunteer. Be as specific as possible, including dates for completion if realistic. Write your actions in ink. There is a far greater feeling of permanence than using pencil.

STEP FIVE Stop Planning and Start Doing! Ideally, start with those actions that will have the biggest impact on your life.

STEP SIX As soon as you have taken action, place a tick next to the action. It is great to see your progress. Do something to reward yourself for having made a difference in your life!

DESIDERATA

Go placidly amid the noise and haste and remember what peace there may be in silence.

As far as possible, without surrender, be on good terms with all persons. Speak your truth quietly and clearly and listen to others, even the dull and ignorant; they too have their story.

Avoid loud and aggressive persons, they are vexations to the spirit.

If you compare yourself with others, you may become vain and bitter; for always there will be greater and lesser persons than yourself.

Enjoy your achievements as well as your plans.

Keep interested in your own career, however humble; it is a real possession in the changing fortunes of time.

Exercise caution in your business affairs; for the world is full of trickery but let this not blind you to what virtue there is; many persons strive for high ideals; and everywhere life is full of heroism.

Be Yourself.

Especially, do not feign affection.

Neither be cynical about love; for in the face of all aridity and disenchantment, it is perennial as the grass.

Take kindly the counsel of the years, gracefully surrendering the things of youth.

Nurture strength of spirit to shield you in sudden misfortune but do not distress yourself with imaginings. Many fears are born of fatigue and loneliness.

Beyond a wholesome discipline, be gentle with yourself. You are a child of the universe, no less than the trees and the stars; you have a right to be here, and whether or not it is clear to you, no doubt the universe is unfolding as it should.

Therefore be at peace with God, whatever you conceive God to be, and whatever your labours and aspirations.

In the noisy confusion of life, keep peace with your soul. With all its sham, drudgery and broken dreams, it is still a beautiful world.

Be careful.

Strive to be happy.

BEING
OPEN

*Exercise caution in your business
affairs; for the world is full of
trickery but let this not blind you to what
virtue there is; many persons strive
for high ideals; and everywhere
life is full of heroism.*

THE VETERAN

Shock radiated from the stunned faces of the two young fire fighters. The car had obviously gone out of control at great speed. The five or six rolls before hitting the large tree had spread debris over a dusty stretch of country road. Enmeshed in the twisted metal was the body of the driver.

'Cut him out,' barked the station officer, determined to throw his rookies in at the deep end. The discomfort of the inexperienced men was obvious as the metal pieces surrounding the deceased fell away under the determined grip of the 'jaws of life'.

The novice fire fighters glanced nervously towards an ambulance which had just arrived. As the last of the metal was removed, a powerful figure swung from the front seat of the ambulance. His weather-beaten face seemed to have etched upon it every one of the twenty-six years he had given to the ambulance service. As he set about the routine of picking up the deceased, his considerable experience alerted him to the concern on the faces of the untried fire fighters. Among the newly initiated, apprehension was a common response in dealing with road death. Although they used the term 'deceased', they were still concerned about 'hurting' the man as they extricated his body.

With a gentleness that belied his appearance, the ambulance officer faced the two novices and quietly said, 'Come on, fellers. Let's look after this gentleman with as much dignity as we can.' His kindly words seemed to drive a shaft of confidence into the fire fighters, who immediately snapped into action and assisted the ambulance officers.

As they left their first operation a few hours later, the young fire fighters felt a sense of purpose few people outside the emergency services can understand. It came not from being brave or tough, but from having managed at a scene that will become common to their calling. Their success came not from any preparation they received in their training, but from the softly spoken words and the sensitivity of an ageing veteran; words of support to assist them to do a job so often characterised by the senseless waste of human lives.

Michael Tunnecliffe

Be sensitive to other people's feelings –
it brings out the best in them.

THE BUTTERFLY
HOUSE

Late autumn in London is characterised by a special kind of light. In mid-afternoon the light softens, dimmed by a golden then mauve haze. The tree-lined streets are littered with leaves: some scattered, some swept up in mounds against fences and gutters, others swirling in eddies.

During the autumn of 1988 I was enjoying my carefully planned overseas experience. Like hundreds of other Australians, I was on a working holiday. I had worked through spring and summer and was planning to work part of the winter before escaping to bright clear skies and warmth. I hadn't decided where in Europe, anywhere but London in the depths of winter, that much was certain.

One evening I went to Richmond, a beautiful leafy town with Edwardian terraces which has now been absorbed into the suburbs of greater London. I had a strange job this autumn, selling rather ordinary paintings door-to-door. Everybody I worked with was a traveller with the identical aim: to earn enough money for that elusive plane ticket to somewhere else.

The weather was chilly and leaves were whipping around my ankles. It was now dark and my folder was heavy; I wanted to be indoors. I knocked at the next house.

A small, spritely, elderly lady with startling eyes answered. I could tell immediately that she was the sort of woman who was happy to talk to anyone. If she knew them, well and good; if she didn't well, she would prattle on all the same. But I didn't mind. She invited me in and I accepted. When people opened their doors to me I always felt privileged that they were allowing me a glimpse of their lives. It was the one aspect of my strange job I really quite liked.

The passageway was very dim and I could smell kerosene. As my eyes adjusted to the light I became aware of butterflies, hundreds of them, all over the walls. The woman ushered me into an equally dim room; here the smell of kerosene was much stronger. An elderly man sat huddled in a vinyl chair near the orange glow of the heater. He offered me a chair. His voice sounded weary and his eyes, unlike those of his wife, were dull.

This room too was filled with butterflies, along the mantel and over the walls. 'Do you collect butterflies?' I asked, thinking this was certainly one of the oddest houses I had ever been inside. 'Oh no!' the old man protested. 'I couldn't kill butterflies, that would be *far* too cruel.' I looked closely. These were butterflies made from feathers and paper, many were cut-outs from breakfast cereal boxes.

The woman was keen to see my paintings and she exclaimed with delight as I drew each one out. I didn't expect the couple to buy any. I doubted anything could upstage their butterfly collection. So I settled for conversation and a viewing. The old man was pleasant but seemed unmoved. 'Life has no meaning for me I'm afraid,' he said suddenly. 'I am merely living out my days.' I was momentarily annoyed. I had experienced this 'one foot in the grave' attitude before; perhaps it was the onset of another dreary winter that made people dour. A gentle touch of humour might help. But before I could speak, the old man began to tell me about his daughter, Margaret.

Margaret was born severely disabled – both physically and intellectually. The old man described how he and his wife had fed, bathed and changed their daughter every day of her life. Well into their seventies, they were still caring for her at home. They never had a sign from Margaret that she knew who they were. On the few occasions they sought respite care they did discover they had some mysterious bond with their daughter. If someone else looked after Margaret, she became inconsolable.

The old man faced a terrible dilemma. Both he and his wife were growing frail and he feared that if one died the other would never be able to cope with Margaret alone. Institutional care for their daughter was not an option. No matter how caring or competent the staff, Margaret would most certainly die of a broken heart.

Calmly, one night, he made his decision. 'I put my daughter to sleep,' he said.

I felt my body stiffen: no breath, no heartbeat, no movement. My thoughts became crowded. Here I was sitting opposite a man who had killed his daughter. The shock of the confession, however, soon dissolved into great compassion for the old man. He had freed his only child by suffocating her. To him it was an act of immense love and kindness, not malice; yet in the eyes of the law this man was a murderer.

'It was in all the papers,' his wife said excitedly, handing me a bunch of clippings. Margaret's death and her father's subsequent trial for murder at the Old Bailey had been a landmark case. The plight of thousands of carers who sacrifice their lives to care selflessly for their disabled children had finally been thrust into the open by this tragic yet courageous act.

A small chill ran through me as I read the clippings. Margaret and I were the same age. The cruel irony of her captivity and my freedom did not escape me, nor, I suspect, did it escape the old man.

I also understood why life held no meaning for him. Despite her severe disabilities, Margaret had been his reason for living and now she was gone. The old man was content to live out his suspended sentence for manslaughter in a vinyl chair in an airless room.

Walking out into the dark street some time later, I was greeted by leaves whirling and slapping at my ankles. I felt revived as the cold air hit my face. But I also felt changed. I knew I would never forget my chance encounter with the couple in the butterfly house.

Dennice Collett

A NOTE FROM DENNICE: This is a true story. However, the name of the daughter has been changed.

Search beneath people's actions
to learn their true intentions –
do they act out of love?

YOU ARE SO BEAUTIFUL

Cancer, when it gets out of control, is nasty.

My wife was a beautiful young woman who enjoyed the outdoors, walking and staying fit and healthy. That was all before the malignant melanoma (the worst form of skin cancer) had developed into its advanced stages.

In June 1991, Linda was thirty-three with a three-year-old son and a five-year-old daughter. She'd been more or less confined to her bed for the past two or three months. You can imagine how pale she looked having not really had a chance to enjoy the sun. The cancer was evident in visible tumours and growths; she had a particularly large tumour in her neck. To say she was thin was an understatement.

As the disease continued to advance, Linda had many visitors. They brought her flowers and, in their own way, said their last goodbyes. Just about everyone walked in the house quietly, spoke softly and tried not to create a disturbance or disrupt the tranquillity of our home.

Diseases such as cancer do give people the chance to catch up with old friends, talk about all the important things in life and to say 'I love you'. I've learnt people like to say goodbye when a person is dying. It makes the visitor feel good, but not necessarily the patient. After a dozen of these solemn visitors, Linda found the lack of hope they displayed totally disheartening. What she needed were friends who just wanted to see her as Linda, not people who needed to visit her because she was dying.

On 10 June 1991, about three weeks before Linda passed away, she had a beautiful experience that stayed with her till her death. Two good friends came to visit, Peter and Pearl Sumner. Peter was completely blind for the majority of his adult life and certainly long before Linda had met him. Due to the benefits of modern medicine, Peter had a cornea transplant and after the operation had about 85 per cent vision in one eye. The success of the surgery was such a wonderful 'good news story' that Peter, Pearl and their seeing-eye dog Luther were interviewed on a morning news show. They came to our home by taxi directly from the television studio.

I remember the day as clearly as if it were this morning. We walked down the centre hallway of our home and turned left at the end of the hall into the bedroom. Linda was resting and just gently opened her eyes enough to recognise Peter and Pearl. As Peter stepped into the bedroom, he burst into exuberance and enthusiasm like a four-year-old child. He kept saying, 'Linda, you're so beautiful! You are so beautiful!' It was the most uplifting visit Linda had experienced in her entire life!

After about three-quarters of an hour, Peter and Pearl left

our home, but their spirit, their love and their joy stayed behind. During those last few months it had seemed that every person who visited Linda (doctors, nurses, home-care helpers, friends, neighbours and relatives) saw a dying young mother with two children. Everyone, that is, except Peter and Pearl. They saw how beautiful Linda was, how beautiful her spirit was. Even in such a difficult situation, Peter and Pearl saw beauty. When you think about it, it is possible to see beauty in every person and every situation, even in a dying mum with two young children.

Peter and Pearl, we love you.

Daniel Johnson

Look for the beauty in everyone you meet.

SNAKE'S EYES

Few people who have ever lived and worked in India would have remained unaffected by it. India is still to many western eyes the quintessential place of mystery and, to many, misery.

Almost half a lifetime ago I was sent to India to work and I took my very young family. I was familiar with Vietnam and Malaysia and we had just been living in Papua New Guinea for some years so I don't suppose the cultural shock affected us as much as it would most people. Nevertheless, prior to heading down to the legendary hill station Ootacamund where we were to be stationed, we spent two weeks getting acclimatised and briefed in New Delhi. We had a guided tour, by hair-raising Sikh taxi, of most of new and old Delhi, as well as the obligatory trip to Agra to see the Taj Mahal and the Red Fort.

A short distance from Delhi is India's answer to the leaning tower of Pisa – a sort of little brother, as it were. It is called the

Qutab Minar. It is a very old and somewhat uncertainly leaning Islamic tower from around the Mogul period. In its vicinity is a smooth iron pillar that resembles a cannon mounted upright. The difference is that it is solid and, from memory, some 10 metres in height. Its origins are lost in antiquity. Certainly no one knows how it got there.

Many legends have grown up around the iron pillar and it has been the subject of speculation in many reputable and often less than reputable books. One of the legends concerns the life of anyone who can stand with their back to the pillar and extend their arms back around the pillar and have their fingers touch on the other side. Being reasonably tall, long-armed and fairly fit and supple in those days, I was able to perform the feat. My doing so brought whoops of approval from our Sikh taxi driver and we were immediately surrounded by dozens of gesticulating children and beggars and, of course, the ubiquitous fortune-tellers and soothsayers.

As we were heading for the taxi to get away from the milling crowd, a singular elderly man with the usual four-days growth, a greasy turban and an equally greasy dhoti detached himself from the crowd. He looked for all the world like the wild-eyed, grey-bearded loon from *The Ancient Mariner* as he grasped my hand. 'Where are you going, Snake's eyes?' I was incensed, only to be told by the Sikh driver that it was meant as a compliment – snakes' eyes are supposedly lucky. The old man demanded that I wait while he told my fortune. But I felt very uncomfortable and resisted (our four-year-old was getting frightened and I was carrying our ten-month-old in my arms). Besides, the driver also seemed to think it was a good idea to go. And yet, despite his wild eyes, there was something inexplicably serene about my accoster. Finally, he let my hand go and said quietly, 'Sahib will understand when I write down his mother's name.' He stood away from me and pulled out an ancient crumpled envelope and the stub of a pencil. Laboriously, he began to write. When he handed me the envelope, there in unformed printing, with only the 'R' back to front, was the name 'Florence'. There was no way that such identification could have been found on my person. My mother was thousands of miles away in Australia and rarely was she ever called Florence, certainly never by me. But make no mistake, Florence was her name.

I must have gone a pale shade of grey but despite my wife's curiosity, I wasn't going to hang around. I can still see the old fortune-teller looking at me disappointedly and I often wonder what he may have told me about the last twenty-five years.

At the time I was a person of fairly well established religious beliefs (I probably still am) but this incident upset my equilibrium and all the old certainties suddenly gave way. Here was something at once utterly inexplicable. It had happened to me and no amount of rationalising can indicate anything other than the work of extra-ordinary psychic forces. No other event since has done as much to convince me of the ultimate interconnectedness of our lives, indeed of this whole world, with something entirely beyond our rationali-sation. And the understanding, or at least the use, of these forces is vested in a semi-literate old beggar half a world away.

Peter Stokes

Be open and nonjudgemental –
life's teachings can come
to you in disguise.

THE UNLIKELY
LOVE LETTER

In early 1942 I received a letter from an unknown soldier, a sergeant in Darwin. The letter explained how he'd been on guard duty with a friend of mine who had shown him a photo of me (my friend had taken it before leaving home). At that exact moment an air raid warning had sounded so the photo was thrust into the sergeant's pocket. That night he wrote a letter to that photo – a letter of sadness in one way (perhaps written out of loneliness and a silent fear of what lay ahead), but also a letter of love and warmth.

I was already writing to several friends in the forces, as were so many of the girls during that era. I put the letter aside, but because of his sincerity and honesty I resolved to answer it sometime in the future. This would never happen as, in February 1942, these men were overcome by the Japanese and taken prisoner – 2/21st Battalion, Gull Force, were lost to communication for the next three and a half years.

When the war ended, the friend who had taken the photo was dead, along with hundreds of others in that notoriously cruel camp. I took it for granted that my sergeant of the love letter was also dead and endeavoured to get on with life and forget those sad years.

In 1951 I was walking back to my office in Melbourne when the lights changed at a street crossing. A gentleman who was caught trying to beat the lights was confronted by a young police-man on duty and told to get back on the footpath. Angry at being stood over after his wartime experiences, the gentleman stamped his foot back onto the footpath and to my surprise landed on my instep laddering my stocking and drawing a little blood. The said gentleman apologised profusely and, as we walked towards my office, he begged to be allowed to replace the stockings at a meet-ing at the Mitre Tavern the next evening.

We were now at my office door, so I agreed to the meet-ing in great haste. As he turned to leave he smiled and gave me his name. It was the same name as my secret letter writer of 1942. I could hardly contain myself. I still had the letter, though how I'll never know – many others had been put down during house moves and tidy-up times.

Next night at the tavern he gave me a new pair of stockings and I gave him the letter. At first it did not mean anything to him (how could it after three and a half years of cruelty and starvation?) but after reading it through it all came back to him. Later that evening as we looked at each other, something told us it was all meant to be – the coincidence was so strong and despite all those years in-between we were both still single. We were married within a year.

On the occasion of our fortieth wedding anniversary celebration, given to us by our son and daughter, I read that famous letter, now fifty years old, to a large gathering of good friends. (Some of these friends, although enjoying the story over the years, were perhaps a little doubtful about the existence of the letter!) So there was the proof, to touch and marvel at – the letter that, with God's help, brought two people together who otherwise might never have met.

Joan Lupson

Be alert – coincidences can have
purpose and meaning.

MY SOUL MATE

Having never married and still being single in my late thirties was not a problem for me. However, my family and some of my friends had more trouble accepting this than I did. I had a busy, interesting life, a great circle of close friends, the ability to travel, the children of friends and family to spoil and love, plus I'd built a successful business. I didn't have the time (I thought) or the need for anyone else in my life.

One Friday the thirteenth I discovered I was wrong. I'd just finalised buying a unit and was meeting friends for drinks. Meeting a man was not on my agenda, but that day my life took a new direction because I subconsciously followed an old principle my mother had instilled in me: 'Never judge a book by its cover'.

My friends introduced me to a man who was financially stricken due to a business loss, unemployed and worse, he smoked! Definitely not my type. From what I'd heard he'd been a high-flier of the eighties with lots of cash (not my type either) and was now at the bottom of the pile. However, after one meeting I knew this man would be very important in my life.

What I saw was what I describe as my 'tree'. A tree without any leaves, bare to the trunk. He was his true self, without all the trimmings upon which society makes its judgements; he had humility, kindness and goodness. Today he has grown and is still blooming, but the trunk of goodness is still there: his wonderful sense of humour, generosity of spirit, romantic nature and loving acceptance of me for who I am.

I had met my soul mate. We married on the thirteenth, eighteen months later. He is my true friend, my lover and my husband.

'Never judge a book by its cover.' Thanks, Mum.

Jenny Keat

Look beyond power, prestige and personal possessions to find true love.

PARADISE

When I first met Charlie he was already an old man. 'G'day, I'm Charlie and this is Pip,' he said, pointing to his Border collie as he handed me one of the two stubbies he carried with him. 'My camp's just down the track a bit.'

That introduction took place about fifteen years ago at my mountaintop retreat where my pampered but frenetic city life gives way to weekends of physical toil and strenuous walks by day, and nights centred around a roaring open fire and abyssal sleep.

Our first beer together went quickly and fairly quietly, the drinking punctuated only by an occasional belch or 'ahh' of appreciation. I returned the compliment. It was evening and we sat quietly together, squinting through the flames of my fire into the setting sun. We were part of a dark-green mass of jungle-covered mountain whose jagged face cast long shadows into a darkening gorge thousands of feet below. Soon the pin-prick of a billion stars would puncture the blackening canopy overhead.

'Paradise,' I whispered, finally breaking a long silence.

'Yes,' drawled Charlie, 'paradise.' And then he and his mate Pip were gone.

Charlie walked in and out of my mountain life for the next fifteen years, turning up unexpectedly then disappearing for long periods. Never staying long. Never intruding. He led a nomadic life but always returned 'home' to the rugged heights, the monstrous trees and the clear streams and waterfalls of 'our mountain'.

He grew up hunting snakes and other reptiles in the foothills with his father 'when there was more money in their skins than there was in grazing'. He had skin that looked like old leather, most of which was exposed to the elements most of the time. In summer he wore khaki shorts; in winter, khaki shorts and a singlet and, perhaps, on bitterly cold rainy days, a hessian bag draped over his shoulders and drawn around his neck with a strand of twisted wire. He was always barefoot.

I asked him to teach me about the bush. 'Yes,' was all he said. He was at least as economical with his conversation as he was with his dress. We went for long walks. At first I took my small children and their friends in the hope that they might understand how special the old man was and learn to share his love and understanding of the bush. But Charlie farted a lot on our walks and the kids fell about behind him blowing 'raspberries' and pulling faces and so I stopped inviting them. Besides, we were much more mobile without the little buggers and I resolved to pass his knowledge on to them as I learnt.

Then four years ago I moved my family to Melbourne. Our visits to the mountain are now much less frequent. Today I set foot on the place for the first time in twelve months. It's so good to be back! I looked for Charlie's camp but there was no sign of it.

Not seeing him today has left me thinking about our friendship. I recall our first brief introduction around my fire and reflect on his simple lifestyle, his extensive knowledge and how unselfishly and gently he offered them both to me. These warm memories are tainted by a sense that I may never see my old mate again.

Tonight is one of those clear, fresh, still nights that are the stuff of my mountain fantasy when I am away. I join a large group sitting around the fire, my children and their friends, young adults now, fine men and women. Some have visited us many times over the last fifteen years and know the mountain well, but others are with us for the first time.

I listen, unnoticed, as they plan tomorrow: '. . . up early and head out into the national park in time to make it to the Antarctic beech. You know, it was probably a tall tree a thousand years before the birth of Christ. We'll get a good look at some giant figs and stinging trees on the way.'

'And we should be able to cut across country to the falls. They'll be working after all the rain we've had.'

Someone notices me among them.

'Hey, Ranger,' (the cheeky buggers have called me Ranger Brian for many years now) 'come with us and show us how to catch crayfish again.'

'Okay,' I say, thinking that I've eaten too much beans and salad with dinner and that tomorrow I'll be farting like a thirty-bob racehorse.

Gathering around the fire on our first night is always a celebration of family and friends coming together in this remote and beautiful environment. Gradually the chatter and bustle of the day and early evening subsides until each of us is left in stillness to soak up the surrounding grandeur in our own way.

'Paradise,' someone whispers, finally breaking a long silence.

'Yes,' I drawl, 'paradise.' And then I'm off to bed.

Brian Beirne

The least likely teacher might
offer you the most to learn.

CLASH OF
CULTURES

In World War II the Australian Army base camps in the Middle East were in Palestine, near the ancient city of Gaza. We carried out training mainly in the sand-dune country along the Mediterranean coast.

One day I was leading a small group on an exercise near the historic Biblical town of Askelon. I was interested to see the town for its history, but also for another reason – because of the special kind of onion brought back from there by the Crusaders centuries before, and thereafter known by the corrupted name of 'shallot'.

Askelon proved to be a rather decrepit and forlorn Arab village. As we approached it along a narrow track we overtook a group which was a common sight at that time: in front, an Arab farmer riding a small donkey with his feet almost touching the ground, and trudging along behind him, his wife with an enormous bundle of sticks on her head.

At this point my sergeant, formally a Clerk of Courts in Broken Hill, suddenly dashed forward and, with many unprintable Australian oaths, threw the bewildered Arab from his donkey and installed thereon his shrieking wife. He then ordered the now furious Arab to pick up the bundle of sticks, gave the donkey a smack on its rear with his bayonet, and sent the small cavalcade in its altered order off down the path towards Askelon.

I mentioned to him afterwards that his piece of modern knight errantry was commendable but certainly misdirected, as the poor women would, without doubt, be severely beaten when they reached home, in retribution for her husband's deep humiliation. Adapting or reinterpreting the Koran was likely to take quite a long time.

'I should have given the bastard a proper thumping,' was his reply.

We have not advanced much. The accepted doctrine in many a TV drama is still that a difference of opinion or belief is best settled by a blow from a fist or a shot from a gun.

Cultures are in collision all over the globe, but there is little sign anywhere of the kind of mutual tolerance and understanding that is critical to peaceful coexistence.

It is an arresting thought that, just possibly, on this crucial matter in the future of the planet, Australia may be able to give a lead to the rest of the world.

Sir Rupert Hamer

*Strive to see every situation from the
other person's point of view.*

MRS FITTLER'S
EGGS

My dad owned and operated the general store in the town where I grew up. Every January, Mum and Dad would pack up and head for the old Coogee Bay Hotel in Sydney. They would stay up there while Dad did his buying for the next year from a wholesaler named Hoffnung.

The year I turned seventeen they set off for Sydney as usual, leaving a manager in charge of the store. They left me there too, waiting for my chance to make my first executive decision. After all, I reasoned, I had learnt a lot about business just by being there and helping around the shop. I was eager to prove I could handle things just as well as he could – maybe even better! I was a seventeen-year-old time bomb, just waiting to explode.

At last my opportunity came. One Tuesday I was left in charge for a few hours. And every Tuesday for the past twenty years, Mrs Fittler had come into the store to sell my father a dozen eggs.

Now you must understand that supply and demand had nothing to do with this transaction. It was just something Mrs Fittler did. Every Tuesday she came into town and sold Nicholas Malouf a dozen eggs. So there I was, in charge. The eggs were fresh but my relationship with Mrs Fittler was rotten. We had just never got on.

I watched her walk in, her face becoming less friendly when she saw that it was me ('that young upstart Doug') behind the counter. In that instant I knew what I was going to do. Here was my chance to show who was boss.

She walked up to the counter and held out her package. 'Good morning,' she said. 'Here are your eggs.'

Poor Mrs Fittler. She hadn't realised yet that she was dealing with Doug Malouf, the hard-nosed businessman and master negotiator. I knew we already had plenty of eggs. I was in a position of strength. So I let her have it right between the eyes: 'We don't want your eggs.'

She didn't seem to notice the crushing blow I'd dealt her. She just fixed me with one unblinking eye: 'Where's your father? He's been buying my eggs for twenty years.'

This was my moment of truth. I had the power to make decisions and I was going to use it. 'My father is in Sydney . . . and I'm the boss. And we don't need your eggs.'

She looked at me again without any signs of emotion. She still didn't seem to realise that I'd won.

'Is that your final word?'

'Yes,' I said.

My cousin Betty in accounts had been watching what was happening. I looked across at her, expecting to see a new respect on her face for my decisive action. Instead, she was smiling at me. But it wasn't a triumphant sort of smile, it was more . . . pitying.

Mrs Fittler walked across to her. 'Betty, I'd like you to make up my account . . . and the Cassidys' and the Jarridays' and all the other Fittler accounts. It'll save them a trip.'

Have you any idea what it's like to be seventeen and to have cost your father's business its best five accounts, plus another six that weren't bad either? Believe me, a wisdom-tooth extraction without anaesthetic looks attractive by comparison. Mrs Fittler clearly didn't understand the laws of supply and demand. She didn't notice that I was in a position of negotiating strength. She just closed eleven accounts and left the store.

Betty was very supportive. 'Just wait till your father gets back,' she said. 'He'll kill you.'

Actually, he didn't kill me. He was very understanding. He discussed the matter calmly, and outlined the options available to me.

'Get those accounts back,' he said, 'or don't bother to come home.'

When I got off my bike and walked up to Mrs Fittler's front door, there she was framed in the doorway. The theme from *High Noon* filled the room behind her. Things didn't look good. I didn't even have to open my mouth.

'Your father sent you, didn't he?'

I nodded.

'Let me tell you something, son. I'm coming back to your father's store. But it's only because he's such a good man. I wouldn't want to hurt him because he's got a fool for a son.'

What could I say?

'There are the eggs,' she said. And she was right. The eggs were there. The same eggs she'd brought in three weeks ago, wrapped in the same newspaper. You didn't need to be able to see them to know they were there. I took a long look at them.

'Well, make up your mind,' she said. 'Do you want them or not?'

She had me, and she knew it. The master negotiator had been beaten. I picked them up delicately and turned to go. She put her hand on my arm to stop me and handed me another parcel.

'Here's two dozen more for the last two weeks. Make sure your father gets them . . . all of them.'

When I got home from Mrs Fittler's, my father underlined the lesson I had learnt. 'Always remember that the customer is your business,' he said, disposing of the eggs. 'The moment you stop giving customer service is the moment you don't have a business.'

You see, what I hadn't understood was that buying Mrs Fittler's eggs was not a business transaction. The purchase showed that Dad wasn't just a shopkeeper. He was part of the community, giving as well as taking. Those eggs represented the relationship of mutual trust and respect he shared with all his customers.

So that's what I learnt. Trust is the basis for prosperity in business. If your customers trust you they won't be one-sale wonders. They'll keep coming back. And they'll bring their friends.

What happened to me might be excusable because I was only seventeen. And it is easy to be wise about it thirty years later. But I still see business people behaving in much the same way in their contacts with their clients. So remember to keep your eyes open for Mrs Fittler. Sooner or later she's going to walk into your office. And when she does, be sure that you buy her eggs.

Doug Malouf

Build your relationships on mutual trust and respect.

A Friend Indeed

I was the oldest student in the university classroom, having gone back to full-time study at the age of thirty-one. I was at least ten years older than most other students in my year.

Because people naturally group with others of their own age and background, I felt very left out when we had to form groups to complete our first marketing assignment. Then, quite suddenly, I was asked to join a group of three other students to complete the project. It was Wendy who asked me to join; an energetic, twenty-year-old Singaporean girl. She had noticed me sitting alone, and although I didn't know her, this small gesture indicated to me a caring person.

Although we were from extremely different backgrounds, we kept in contact regularly and over time our friendship grew. I graduated in November 1994, but Wendy stayed on at university in 1995 for two more semesters.

One day I had a call from a very distressed Wendy. Not wishing to burden her older family in Preston or her student friends for accommodation, Wendy had agreed to rent a small room in a house owned by a single mother in Hawthorn. The woman had advertised for an overseas student in the hope of earning some rent to help with the support of her small child.

I knew that Wendy would be a very considerate house guest but when she complained to me about the extreme restrictions placed on her freedom at Hawthorn, not to mention her landlady's mood swings, I suspected that her environment was less than ideal for her final year of study.

After discussions with my husband, we both agreed to ask Wendy if she would like to live with us until she had graduated and was ready to return to Singapore. Wendy shyly agreed, so it was off to collect her belongings.

It was so refreshing to have Wendy live with us. We shared many happy times together: cooking Asian food, introducing her to friends and family, throwing parties, seeing movies, having Sunday brunches at the local, and sharing news at the end of each day. We just enjoyed being together. Wendy brought laughter and life to our home.

Soon after she came to stay, we discovered that Wendy was immensely talented musically. Her strict upbringing was evident in the way she concentrated on playing classical pieces on the piano. She explained that as a child she had been instructed by a master from the Conservatorium of Music in London. So strict were the masters on their pupils that any mistakes would be punished with a sharp wrap across the knuckles. Wendy soon learnt to avoid this humiliation (and pain!) by becoming an excellent pupil. However, her skill could only be sharpened by hour upon hour of practice (usually under the watchful eyes of her parents).

Notwithstanding these experiences, music is Wendy's passion and we shared many nights entertaining ourselves and others (whether they yawned or not!) around the piano.

Wendy graduated in August 1995 and left Australia soon after. Much to her credit, she engaged an accounting position in Singapore before departing. We write to each other regularly. I miss her a great deal.

People praised us for our generosity in offering Wendy a place to stay. I don't see it that way. Wendy gave us so much more by just being there. She 'unfocused' us and helped us see fun and humour in the simplest of things. After so many years of work and study, she taught me to lighten up and enjoy 'the now'. I feel privileged to be her friend.

Sharon Thomson

Make a new friend; you never know
what you may learn.

I Do What
I Am

I can still remember walking around school, lonely, confused and shy. I couldn't understand how the other kids could make friends and I couldn't. Even worse, I knew they were talking about me behind my back, laughing about me. I don't blame them; I had become a pretty unhappy kid. My father had lost all his money, and he had become extremely depressed. My mother, who had narrowly escaped the Holocaust, found it very hard to cope. I didn't have a choice; I grew up overnight and my adolescence vanished. I lost my confidence, my friends and my self-esteem. No wonder I was an easy target at school.

That was many years ago. In the meantime I studied, then I married, had three children and then studied again, so that I could become financially independent. Early in my marriage, it became apparent that I had married a man who was like my father.

I kept most of my suffering secret; living with a manic

depressive can be funny in retrospect, but devastating while it is happening. As a child I had learnt that you keep unpleasant things secret and that family problems are not to be advertised. I believed that I was just being loyal. I kept quiet about my husband's difficulties for most of my marriage.

I didn't realise that secretiveness led to violence and abuse. It isolated me from support and care. Those were very difficult years and I coped on my own.

As a young mother I had some free time to spare. I did some voluntary work in the school where I had gone and where my children were attending. A year later I was employed as a school psychologist. The school had over 2000 students and for a number of years I was the only psychologist. I realised then that I hadn't been the only shy, scared and lonely kid there. It was still happening today.

My marriage broke up and then I was really on my own. A year later my eldest daughter died from a genetic illness. She was aged nineteen. There are many problems in life that one can sublimate, deny or minimise. Losing a child needs immediate attention. One's life is devastated; everything disintegrates.

I threw myself into my work, developing the groups with shy children and slowly building a now successful private practice. I joined committees and worked for others in a voluntary capacity. I did extra training and kept myself very busy.

I can remember clearly sitting one afternoon at my desk, the sun streaming in through the window. I was writing a script for a video. Suddenly I was forced to put everything together, to create a proper perspective. What I discovered was that I needed to juxtapose my personal life and the pain I had experienced with my training and practice. Within a few hours I had developed a model of relating that I am now using constantly in my work. It is not only unique, but simple, and I utilise the wisdom of my model daily.

Where does my personal life end and my professional life begin? In the end, we are a sum of our life experiences. Out of the ashes of my grief I learnt that you can't deny your feelings; you need to understand why you feel that way, rather than blame yourself or torture yourself with guilt. After many years of self-neglect and self-denigration I needed to rebuild my self-esteem and do things differently and find moments to care for myself.

I learnt that keeping secrets is bad and that I needed people, and therefore I needed to relate more effectively. As a basically shy person this has not always been easy, but I know what to do and I try to practise, although I don't always try hard enough. Sometimes I force myself and sometimes it comes easily. At the same time I learnt that I need to deal with difficult people, because they are there, whether they are mad, bad or just having a difficult day, and they can take away my power, if I let them.

When my daughter died, I was able to discover what true friendship means, and I felt supported by those friends who were close or those who wanted to care and to help. Finally I learnt that we are not just human beings, but we are also social beings and that I love needing people and giving to them. I love my family and my friends and I care for the people I work with. Thus, my final lesson was that we all need people and we need to have a support network, if we are to survive in this life.

What I learnt is the basis of my psychological model, the 'Secrets of Relating'. It has been described as 'idiot proof' and certainly everyone I work with, in my practice, in lectures or when I write, from young kids to successful professional or business people, can understand, learn and practise it.

I resent the price I paid for this model, but I respect the understanding my loss has brought me. As a result, I am very different. I have grown, in many new directions, and used my personal experience together with my knowledge as a psychologist and presenter. Being able to help others, as a professional psychologist, using the pain and deeper understanding of my unique personal experiences, constantly provides me with a special measure of satisfaction.

You may ask 'But where are you today?' and the answer is not simple. I survive; I cope. That is my major achievement. I love my family, my friends, my work and my dogs. For a long time I did anything to keep busy. Now I know my limits and am beginning to care for myself, instead of just care for others, and whenever I am in pain I am learning to be loving to myself.

Evelyn Field

Discover friendship and love by sharing.

THE JOHN AND
MILKA STORY

The year was 1964, I was not quite forty and my eyes had been opened to what tourism and the free exchange of peoples could mean. So smitten was I that seven years earlier I had abandoned daily journalism to become the chief executive of Australia's fledgling national tourist organisation.

There was at this time an august body known as the International Union of Official Travel Organisations. This mouthful of a name – IUOTO for short – was the Geneva-based world tourism body with a membership of 110 countries. It is now known, more simply, as the World Tourism Organisation (WTO).

One of my early problems was to persuade the Australian government to join IUOTO and permit me to play a part in its growth. Whether we were from Moscow or the Middle East, a jaded veteran from western Europe or a wide-eyed tourism disciple from Australia, we met regularly and went about our task of freeing up the world with missionary zeal.

The age of the jet had just arrived and overnight the world had shrunk. The tourism professionals in IUOTO were ahead of their time in recognising this and, as proof that their burgeoning industry was ready to straddle the globe, chose Bangkok as the venue for the 1964 General Assembly and me as the new president (the first to come from so far away as the Southern Hemisphere).

Some 300 of us gathered in Bangkok to ponder what we could do to open up the world so we could all gain more from this dollar-rich business. After a heavy first day in the chair bewitched and confused by discussion in four languages, I was ready that evening for a relaxing dinner. A friend, John Paine, head of international relations for Pan American in New York, asked me to join him.

We met in the hotel lobby and were on our way to the restaurant when John saw a woman sitting by herself in the lounge. A gregarious type, John went over to her, reminded her we were all in Bangkok as delegates together and suggested she join us for dinner. Her acceptance could not have been more effusive. 'Thank you, thank you, thank you,' she said. 'You've no idea what this means to me. I've never been so far away before or felt so lonely and homesick.'

Her name was Milka Kufrin. A pleasant, handsome woman in her early forties, she was the Minister for Tourism in the former Yugoslavia. Her country was then very much on the communist outer as the renegade which refused to become a Soviet satellite. A tough cookie when she needed to be, she was very much of the same independent spirit. A national hero for her deeds as an eighteen-year-old serving with Marshal Tito's partisans in the war, she was rewarded by being made her country's tourism minister.

At that time, the Cold War was at its most bitter and the feeling between east and west was at a razor's edge. There was next to no tourism across the abyss and about the only fraternisation was at international parleys like ours. Although a communist country, Yugoslavia sat in the middle. But this was of little concern to John and Milka. They got along famously as individuals.

At our final dinner at the end of the week, I happened to sit again with both of them. I could not help overhearing their conversation.

'Why do so few of your people visit my country, John?' Milka asked.

'I'll tell you why,' John replied. 'I've been to Yugoslavia and it's beautiful. But scenery means nothing if Americans feel insecure. Tourists see you as a communist country stifled by red tape, with poor service and lousy hotels. There are plenty of easier countries for them to go to.'

'What can I as minister do to change things?' she asked.

'For a start, if you had decent hotels it would help. Americans would be more inclined to go there then. My people will put up with almost anything if they have a room to go to at the end of the day where they feel comfortable and secure.'

'With all our other priorities, how do I go about building hotels?'

'That's easy,' John replied. 'Leave it to us. We'll get Intercontinental to build them for you. Tourists will quickly follow.'

That was the start of it all and it is exactly what happened. It took a year for Milka to get Tito to agree but he did, finally. And two years later, Intercontinental had built a large hotel in Zagreb followed by two more in other parts of the country. American tourists with their precious dollars as well as tourists from other countries with their badly needed currencies began to swarm in.

This was the dawn of a new era, the first mixing of communism and capitalism through tourism. Soon, other communist countries, jealous of Yugoslavia's independence and sudden economic progress, had learnt the same lesson. Joint hotel projects with western groups were sprouting throughout eastern Europe.

This was the end of the hard line. As more tourists arrived, people from west and east began mixing together. Walls started to crumble and sharp divisions evaporate. People-power had taken over and governments had little option but to take notice and respond.

And so with people from different countries getting to know and understand one another better, wars are further away and the world is a happier place. I like to think John and Milka played a part in this.

Basil Atkinson

A kind word or deed can work miracles.

BUILDING BRIDGES

Like many Australians, I had an understanding that Aborigines had been part of this continent long before Captain Cook and that they had been poorly treated by the early European settlers who had subsequently followed. But that understanding was merely academic, of historical interest, and imposed no imperative upon me to accept any responsibility for the past.

I did, however, recognise that Aborigines and Torres Strait Islanders were among the most disadvantaged of all Australians and that health, education and employment opportunities for them had to be improved. It was with this concern that I accepted the invitation to represent Australian business on the Council for Aboriginal Reconciliation. Of all the decisions I have made, few have been more challenging or more personally enriching.

Simply being exposed to indigenous culture and ancient law, together with my growing respect and understanding of their complexity and relevance to survival in a harsh and unforgiving land, gave me a new perspective on what it means to be Australian. It disclosed the ancient and proud history of a people who sought balance between life and the land that gave life – a history which has much relevance to our society today.

However, I also learnt of another, more recent history of personal deprivation and separation of children taken from their families and taught, quite deliberately, that their culture and spiritual beliefs were of no importance and that they should disregard their values and embrace those of our modern European society. Above all, it was a history of their dispossession from the land that was central to their existence. The dominant outcome of this for many Aborigines was disease, despair, alcoholism and death.

I came to the stark realisation that these stories were not from some time long past; these were stories recalled from personal experience, they were stories of today, of people of my generation.

So, why would any Aborigine who had experienced such extreme trauma entertain the wish to seek reconciliation with other Australians? Of course, I was well aware of the Aborigines of the newspaper headlines who used bitterness to support revenge and even revolution. Clearly, they rejected the notion of reconciliation.

There were, however, others who were driven by a more powerful force that seemed to have its origins deep within their culture and spiritual values. These people embraced the conviction that an understanding of and a respect for all cultures and people would create an environment in which the disastrous events of the past would not be repeated and where continuing injustices could be removed.

While there are many examples, the experience of one Aborigine, in particular, gives me total certainty that the process of reconciliation can be successful in Australia.

Taken from his parents at a very early age to be raised 'for his own good' in a European environment was one of his earliest recollections. So total was that removal from his family and people that he now bears only the name of the railway station from which the government officials took him. He spent years working for white graziers with little formal education. However, despite this separation, he learnt of his cultural heritage and of its imperative that life and land were inseparable. He was often heard to say: 'Until you have spent at least one night in the bush with my people and listened to its stillness, heard our stories and become as one with the land, you cannot begin to understand my culture.'

It became apparent that much of the land of his people had not only been taken away but had been poisoned following the experimental detonation of a number of atomic devices. No longer could his people walk their traditional lands or seek spiritual regeneration from its special places. For four decades he challenged both the British and Australian governments, politically and through the courts, to accept responsibility and to recognise the need for compensation.

Despite these experiences he bears no bitterness. Rather, he carries a determination to rebuild the cultural and spiritual values of his people and to reach out to non-Aboriginal Australians to build a mutual understanding and respect.

From those humble beginnings and an early life of separation and hardship, the broader community has recognised the importance of his work. An Order of Australia, the Citizen of the Year and, more recently, an honorary doctorate from a major university, have all sought to give honour to his achievements. However, regardless of being granted some of the highest awards a nation can give, his commitment remains simple – respect for each individual and their beliefs and respect for the land.

This, of course, is just one personal experience and is by no means unique. Because it is one story among many, it gives me hope. Stories such as this teach us that it is important to not only understand and accept responsibility for the past but also to plan for a better future. For a nation like Australia, which places great store in being modern, developed and sophisticated, we have much to learn from what is arguably the world's oldest culture. We can learn the value of stillness and of listening; of involving all in the process of reaching a consensus; of sustainable consumption that ensures the land continues to give life; of balance; and above all, of care for all in society.

Reconciliation cannot be achieved by legislation or through judicial action. Reconciliation will come from individual citizens changing the way they think and act towards each other.

Within a few years we will conclude the first century of Australia's Federation. If we wish to ensure that our second century achieves unity and equity for all, the spirit of reconciliation must be embraced by all Australians.

Ian Spicer

*Respect the beliefs of others – you will
learn from their wisdom.*

THE LONGEST
TWO HOURS

I was the only woman in a group of about sixty adults and kids that set off for an afternoon kayaking and snorkelling excursion in Hawaii. There were fathers with their children, unaccompanied children and me with my two gorgeous sons, Jim (sixteen) and Hugh (eighteen).

Initially, I refused to take a twin kayak and look after a little girl who was alone. I wanted to enjoy myself, not be a surrogate mum. Anyway, why didn't they ask one of the men? When it looked like she would end up alone, I relented and paired up with Bekky, who was twelve but looked about eight.

My sons were in their own single kayaks and it was rapidly becoming obvious that the organisers were out of their depth with a group this size, especially as the weather was getting wilder by the minute.

Bekky, my sons and I were in the last group to leave the

beach. Even though we didn't have enough masks and fins, we didn't care – we were impatient to leave. Our destination was about 1.5 kilometres off shore, so we paddled fast with the strong off-shore wind and soon joined the others at the snorkelling spot. Our kayaks were tied together in a single cluster and supposedly anchored.

Bekky wanted to go snorkelling and I supported her case (after all, her parents had trusted her to come alone), but the guide, by now hopelessly frazzled, forbade it. Bekky, now a firm friend, was upset but didn't make a fuss.

As there was a shortage of snorkelling gear, my sons, who were in their school swimming team and qualified surf lifesavers, decided to have a swim. I decided not to bother. Some of the previous arrivals were already returning to shore.

No one was looking forward to the return paddle, but it was time to head back. I looked around for my sons. I could not see Jim but did not register the fact that his kayak had also disappeared. Anyway, I knew for certain that he would not have left the group without telling us. At first Hugh laughed it off, then started diving around the area. During this time, Bekky was contained and sensible, perhaps I was too. But when the wind picked up and the sky clouded over, Hugh and I cautiously raised the alarm. Our guide, however, panicked and started to worry about the insurance.

Hugh, sensibly realising that conditions were hopeless for any of us to make a personal search, paddled back to shore to raise the alarm. He was an incredibly fit young sportsman and must have broken all records in his race for the beach, despite the howling offshore wind.

The other kayak clusters had left without knowing our drama. The guide requested that I get 'the others' into shore while he headed out to sea to search. I told him that one man in a kayak would be unlikely to find anything in those conditions, all the time telling myself that Jim was a great swimmer and would be okay. The 'others' were four twin kayaks filled with eight overweight teenage girls. I tied the four kayaks together in single file behind mine, and Bekky and I set out for shore. After only ten minutes the others were whingeing about sore arms and how they were never going to make it. I must admit it did seem an impossible task against the wind and the rain. Counting 'one-two, one-two' occasionally got them paddling with some sort of rhythm, but mostly it was a case of us towing them.

Underneath all the physical strain I was aware of a deepening fear. My head said Jim was okay but my heart, I confess, was afraid he wasn't. Meanwhile, Bekky was very aware of all that was happening and that little girl never stopped paddling once, even though she was half the size of 'the others'. She also maintained a very positive banter during this extremely difficult time. Without knowing whether Jim was alive or not, Bekky and I paddled for about one and a half hours.

Just before we reached the safety of the shore, Hugh paddled out to meet me. Jim was safe. Apparently, for some unknown reason, the guides had detached Jim's kayak from our cluster and attached it to one that left the snorkelling spot before us. Jim, in the water at the time, looked up and briefly saw his empty kayak being towed into shore. The high waves blocked his view, so he could neither see us behind him, nor the direction of his rapidly disappearing boat. So he did exactly the right thing and swam to the nearest shore and then walked to where the earlier arrivals, now alerted by Hugh, waited. He said it was an easy swim; he'd even beaten his own kayak back into shore.

Hugh took over towing so Bekky and I raced towards the shore. Paddling now seemed so much easier. Back on the beach, my elation at holding both my sons was short-lived; the guide who'd headed out to sea to search for Jim was now lost. Thank goodness they eventually found him, four hours later. By then, of course, their communication and search procedures, both on land and sea, were well and truly exposed.

But the clear-headedness and strength of my sons were also exposed, as was my good fortune to have Bekky on board.

Lyndsey Cattermole

Never underestimate the strength of others.

TAKING ACTION

BEING OPEN

Use this Action Planner to turn the messages in this

chapter into reality in your life. Turn to pages xvi–xvii to

learn the six simple steps you need to know to make the

most of this Action Planner and to enhance your life.

ACTION STEP

Arrange a quiet meal with your partner this week.
Begin the conversation by saying, 'Tell me about . . .'
then shut up and listen!

MY SPECIFIC ACTION STEP

....
....
....
....
....
....

ACTION STEP

For one day, make the conscious decision to see
beauty in every person you meet. Compliment them
if it seems appropriate.

MY SPECIFIC ACTION STEP

....
....
....
....
....
....

ACTION STEP

Pick up the telephone and ring someone you haven't
spoken to in a long time. Ask them how they feel,
then do more listening than talking.

MY SPECIFIC ACTION STEP

....
....
....
....
....
....

ACTION STEP

Go out of your way to meet someone. It may be someone with
whom you have nothing in common. Talk to them until you learn
something new, then thank them for what you have learnt.

MY SPECIFIC ACTION STEP

....
....
....
....
....
....

ACTION STEP

The next time you have a conversation or disagreement with another person that requires you to have a high degree of empathy, in your mind's eye swap places with them and try to represent the other person's position for five minutes. (This is especially effective in manager–employee or parent–child situations.)

MY SPECIFIC ACTION STEP

....

....

....

....

ACTION STEP

Help someone you know in a completely unexpected way.
For example, if you are making lasagne for dinner,
make two and give the extra one away.

MY SPECIFIC ACTION STEP

....

....

....

....

....

....

ACTION STEP

Send a card or a letter to someone you know marking a significant moment you have shared together. They will always have a memento of your special times that they can reflect upon in later life.

MY SPECIFIC ACTION STEP

....
....
....
....
....

ACTION STEP

The next time someone asks you to do something you wouldn't normally do, like go abseiling or try a new cuisine, keep an open mind and ask yourself the question: 'What's the worst thing that can happen?' Then consider the alternative: 'What's the best thing that can happen?'

MY SPECIFIC ACTION STEP

....
....
....
....

KNOWING
YOURSELF

*Nurture strength of spirit to
shield you in sudden misfortune
but do not distress yourself
with imaginings. Many fears are
born of fatigue and loneliness.*

REALISING
SUCCESS

When my wife rang me at my office to ask me to put aside a full day to be with her, my expectations were high. It was a special thing for us to take time out to be together. Nevertheless, when I finally found out what the day was to be about I was aghast. Dianne told me that she was going to jump out of an aeroplane and, even worse, that the training session was less than twenty minutes! She tried to put me at ease by telling me that it was a tandem parachute jump, and that she would be doing it with a highly trained instructor. I'd always been supportive of Dianne in everything she wanted to do, and decided now was not the time to withdraw that support.

However, when we arrived at the airfield and saw the light aluminium aircraft with its open side door and two large 'fans', my confidence took a dive. But then, as I watched and listened to how people were reacting, I eventually realised it was a highly organised and professional outfit and I became more relaxed.

Dianne was hesitant but excited and, after being harnessed up, she got into the plane which took off smoothly and climbed to around 6000 feet. I watched, my binoculars fixed on the side door of the plane, as a small dot emerged. Seconds later the chute opened and down they spiralled to a perfect landing on a gravel patch. I ran to Dianne, who was breathless with excitement: 'That was the greatest experience I've ever had!' As we drove home I asked her what she had really achieved from this experience and she said, 'I've done something I've always wanted to do. It was exciting.'

Later that evening I returned home from a meeting to find Dianne was sitting in a chair with a faraway look in her eyes. I asked her if she was okay. She looked at me and said, 'Didn't you feel the earthquake at around seven o'clock tonight?' I replied that I hadn't as I was on the tenth floor of the Hilton Hotel. Her knees shaking, she stood up and looked at me intensely: 'I realised tonight what I've done.' I returned her gaze, hanging on her every word. She said, 'I realised that today I didn't just jump out of a plane, I busted through a barrier of fear that I've held for years. But more importantly, I realised that the only thing that is stopping me from being whatever I want to be, and doing whatever I want to do, is how I view those situations in my mind.'

Realising that success and happiness are more a state of mind than a state of circumstance helps us to achieve our true potential and to enjoy its evolution for eternity.

Colin Bockman

Expand your thoughts and you will
achieve your full potential.

THE MESSAGE
IN THE
TOOTHACHE

I arrived home after a week-long business trip to discover my husband, James, stoically enduring a painful gum inflammation. The left side of his face was very swollen and his tooth was wobbling dangerously loose in its socket. He had tried everything in his healing repertoire to lessen the constant throbbing, all to no avail. It appeared that his tooth was about to suffer a certain fate — permanent exile from his mouth.

As a psychotherapist successfully incorporating various techniques to access the infinite healing powers of the unconscious mind, I offered my services to him. It was the last chance before the impending visit to the dentist.

As I guided my husband into a relaxed state of mind, he expanded his awareness to make contact with his wise, knowing self. This process was to guide him back to the very first time he made the long-forgotten decision that resulted in his present-day gum inflammation – a decision that was not available to his conscious mind.

He soon became aware of an event that occurred when he was only three years old. His parents were sending him off to spend yet another weekend with his grandmother, as they had done so many times before. James discovered that his 'little boy' was still very angry at being abandoned by his parents. Upon accessing this memory, I assisted him in resolving his ancient, unresolved anger. Thus he was finally able to forgive his parents and restore his inner peace.

Upon completion of the process, I was most anxious to hear about his experience. To the amazement of us both, when he returned from his inner journey not only had the pain totally disappeared but so had the swelling. Even more incredible, the tooth that had been so precariously loose was once again solidly in place in its socket.

Within less than ten minutes, my husband's week-long condition of pain, inflammation and swelling had totally healed. Not a trace of the problem remained. It certainly was a most undeniable experience of the awesome healing power of the body–mind.

My husband's profound transformation was a testimony to the miracle of healing available to all of us if we are willing to release the trapped emotions of past memories. The shadows of those long-forgotten hurts reveal themselves in the present as pain and disease in the body.

Making peace within oneself is certainly the greatest healing balm of all.

Sherrill Sellman

Good health is a choice – access the
awesome power of the body–mind.

Sweet Talking

At three, my son Mark became a stutterer. We worried about it a lot, but then the hesitation, the stumbling and the jumbling of words would disappear for about three months. Three months on and three months off seemed to be the pattern.

Trips to child psychologists and speech therapists over the next twelve years seemed to make very little difference to his speech. It was still three months on, three months off. When it was 'on' it was difficult for him to cope. In primary school he seemed to be able to make adjustments some of the time but we would watch him find ways to manoeuvre his way into silence rather than speech. He was adept at getting his much younger brother to buy tickets at the railway station and the movies for him. We learnt not to finish sentences for him. We learnt to wait patiently until the end of his statement no matter how long that took and how pained and contorted the expression on his face as he forced out a word or phrase. Not every word and phrase was stuttered, of course. Only some. Mark would race through his communication when he was not tripped up by the stutter. That was because he didn't know when he would have to pause and give in to it.

His entire communication was extremely fast, with syllables lost in the battle to stay ahead of the stutter. He made very little eye contact. By the time he was in high school his self-esteem was very low. He chose to sit in the library reading rather than to mix with other boys at recess and lunch times.

Mark was fifteen when we heard of a residential training course which taught stutterers to speak all over again. We were warned that it was a difficult course and that adults often did not succeed so the chances of a fifteen-year-old boy achieving the new 'smooth speech' were not high.

With great trepidation we delivered him to the residential unit at the psychiatric hospital. He was scared and refused to get out of the car. Eventually we had to drag him out and convince him that the course would be of great advantage. It was to last two weeks or so and in that time we were not to contact him. He would contact us when he was permitted. As parents of an isolated, lonely, shy young man we couldn't sleep for worrying about him.

The idea of 'smooth speech' may sound monotonous to you and me. But to the students of the course, it gave a sense of control. The learning of the technique was difficult. The exercises were interminable. The testing after a few days was daunting. Each student was given a tape recorder with a built-in microphone and after hiding it somewhere would have to interview another student. Once they proved that they could speak for four minutes in 'smooth speech' mode without resorting to their old patterns and stuttering, they progressed. Next came interviews and conversations with hospital workers also using a hidden tape recorder. It wasn't just a matter of asking the workers questions, some of the time had to be used by the student to speak as well.

When they were able to pass three of those secretly taped interviews it was time to telephone parents and friends and relatives for secretly recorded conversations. None of us knew that this was happening. To progress to the next stage, the students had to make no mistakes: no stuttering and always 'smooth speech'. Always. If, even once, they made a mistake, it was back to the beginning of the recording process – back to interviewing the other students, then the hospital employees and then parents and friends again. Each day at replay time the students discovered whether they had passed or failed. They lived on a knife-edge of anxiety. Mark apparently did well for a few days until in one conversation with me he made a mistake. The last five days went out the window in that instant. Back to the beginning again, he was told. I hate to imagine the anger and frustration that went through his mind. I cried when he later told me about it. Mark, however, was very determined to succeed. So he did them all over again with his heart pounding during every conversation. Some students never got past this ordeal, gave up and went home.

The following week we received another telephone call. Mark told me what a wonderful success he'd achieved that day. In that second week he'd gone out into the community and secretly taped four minutes of talks with shopkeepers and people on the street. I wondered how he had coped with that task, since he was a very shy boy who avoided personal contact like the plague.

His biggest success, and the finale to the course, was the recording made in a florist shop with the shop assistant. He asked about the price of flowers, the types of flowers available then, how flowers would be sent . . . anything and everything he could think of to fill in six minutes. And all taped secretly. If only that florist realised today how she'd contributed to Mark's new life. If only I could thank her.

Mark was one of the few to pass the course. We were so proud for him. We picked him up at the hospital to be greeted by 'Hello, Mum and Dad' drawled very slowly. But what a wonderful improvement this slow and monotonous speech was over the machine-gun staccato of the conversations we'd been used to.

Today most of you would not pick Mark as a stutterer. His speech has changed dramatically since that training seventeen years ago. He certainly is a deliberate speaker, and has to think carefully about what he says and how he says it, but now he makes good eye contact, can put his ideas across forcefully and is a confident, happy and loving husband and father.

I often congratulate him on his courageous success. He doesn't quite agree: 'Once a stutterer, always a stutterer, Mum.'

Lynn Champion

You can change and improve yourself
if you are determined enough.

EVERY BREATH
I TAKE

I have had asthma all my life. It was diagnosed when I was little more than an infant. I am now in my late forties. Looking back to the bad old days, I really appreciate the advances made in asthma medication. I used to have to swallow some foul-tasting white powder which made me feel ill for hours, and take pills which made me shake. The Aspaxadrine pump, which I used daily, will bring back memories for most asthmatics over forty. This device was a rather complicated affair made of glass and rubber; you poured a solution into it and squeezed the rubber handle to make a vapour. Again, this solution was a real shake-maker.

When I was really ill, I was put on quite long courses of steroids. I was on and off steroids for about eight years and fortunately I did not suffer many side effects. I do have thin skin and bruise very easily now, which my doctor told me is a legacy of the amount of steroids I had to take.

I was one of those weedy, sickly children who are usually portrayed in fiction as the teacher's pet. In fact, I barely knew any teachers because I was bedridden for months at a time, propped up on pillows and wheezing more or less constantly. I missed a lot of school and while I had a good general knowledge, it was always a battle to try and keep up with my class. I was a determined child and I sat for and obtained my Higher School Certificate with the same group I started out with twelve years previously. My school friends remember me as the classmate who was never there and recall they had to pray for my recovery during the times I was particularly unwell. I gather my parents were told by doctors I would be lucky to survive to adulthood.

Most of my early memories are coloured by my chronic asthma. Looking back, I realise how awful it must have been for my parents and the rest of the family; my illness certainly curtailed family activities. Unless my grandparents could look after me, one of my parents always had to stay home, while the other one went out with my brothers and sister. If I was well enough to go out, we could not visit people who had cats or lived in dusty, old houses. On one memorable occasion, when I was taken to afternoon tea in Canberra at the home of the federal leader of the opposition, I disrupted the whole afternoon by having a massive asthma attack after sitting on a couch that was usually occupied by the family cat.

I had scratch tests on my arm and was allergic to nearly everything. From about the age of five until I was thirteen, I had constant respiratory infections, contracted pneumonia a number of times and coughed incessantly. I remember finding life very tiring. I would often sit up half the night wheezing and coughing and then doze on and off during the day. I had no appetite and was very underweight. My father would try and help me put on weight by giving me glasses of Guinness stout.

I kept waiting to grow out of asthma; people kept telling me I would. The years passed and the wheezing lessened, but did not go away. The Aspaxadrine was replaced by a Medihaler, which was replaced by Ventolin. By now I was an expert on asthma medication. At least Ventolin did not make me shake or tremble. I tried swimming at the baths, but I continually picked up ear and throat infections. I tried walking in the early morning, but the cold air would make me cough. So I swam in private pools and walked later in the day. I also bought a bike. I took up yoga and tried meditation. All these activities helped make me stronger, but the asthma stayed with me. When I turned twenty and was still a chronic asthmatic, I decided I might have to learn to live with it for life. This was not a negative reaction, but rather a positive realisation. I decided to beat asthma at its own game.

And I have. I am still classified as a chronic asthmatic, but I describe myself as a controlled asthmatic. I do have the occasional lapse, but overall I stick to a fairly strict program and have done so for many years. I look after myself by eating a balanced diet, staying slim, exercising regularly, getting enough rest and avoiding as many asthma triggers as possible. I think I have increased my resistance to infection, which is one of my major triggers. In the past I would be hospitalised two or three times a year with asthma. I have not been to hospital for some years now, except for a period last year when I had pneumonia.

I would like my experience with asthma to serve as a source of encouragement for others. I have been able to lead a full and active life, which has included two children and a career as a journalist. My emotional attitude towards my asthma is good;

when I do become ill, I no longer see it as the end of the world. I don't force myself to go on as I used to in the past. I increase my medication if necessary, rest, drink lots of liquid and avoid stressful situations whenever possible.

It may have taken a long time, but I now apply common sense to coping with asthma. I see my asthma as a constantly lurking enemy, but an enemy who will never win the battle.

Maria Prendergast

Be committed to self-improvement –
you will lead a healthier,
more enjoyable life.

An 'Open' Marriage

The day my husband said he wanted an 'open' marriage my life changed forever.

To him it was a perfectly reasonable option, to me it was just another term for 'freedom to cheat'. What he really wanted was to be single.

This new arrangement soon destroyed our family life and our twenty-year marriage. My husband came and went like a boarder and every absence was like a knife twisting in my heart; I knew exactly who he was with. I moved out of his bedroom and he moved out of my life. When we did see each other we argued and fought and I became depressed. 'How could he do this to me?' I railed, never thinking to look at myself.

I knew I had to get a divorce but I was not working at the time and was financially dependent on him to care for our three children. So I decided to stay, although poverty and hardship would have been far easier than living this lie.

Life began to lose its meaning as I acted out a 'happy marriage' to friends and family. I spent a lot of time feeling sorry for myself and I lost my confidence and self-esteem. I saw less and less of my husband and began to feel terribly lonely and unloved. Secretly I longed for somebody to hold and love me and I went to bed alone and dared to dream. But I knew that I couldn't possibly attract a man while I was feeling so miserable. Occasionally I went out with single girlfriends, shopping for 'true love'. Not surprisingly our efforts were in vain.

After a year something happened that changed my image of myself. A friend who was keen to try skydiving tried to talk me into going too. The thought of jumping out of an aeroplane terrified me, but I realised I needed a challenge. Perhaps I instinctively knew that facing these external fears would give me the courage to look at my internal fears. I finally did jump and, to my surprise, I loved it.

This spurred me on to look for other physical challenges, so I took up rock-climbing and enjoyed that too. Rock-climbing is a challenging sport that requires total concentration so it is bound to take your mind off personal problems. By taking risks and facing my fears I had grown stronger and my self-esteem and confidence were boosted enormously. I loved the new person I had become and now I also had the confidence and courage to be an individual.

One day, when I was not even looking for love, it came into my life. I met a happy, positive and successful man who was also a very passionate and loving person. 'You are the most beautiful person in the world to me,' he would say. Nobody had ever given me such a compliment. Every time we saw each other we felt great joy and became closer and closer. The love we felt was stronger than any we had experienced before. We soon became so close I was sure we were soul mates. That was more than two years ago and we still feel the same today.

I should thank my ex-husband for tossing me aside. He forced me to look at myself and change. Now I realise I didn't love him completely. Thanks to my ex-husband's actions I have found a real happiness and contentment, and the greatest love of my life.

Anonymous

A NOTE FROM SUE AND DANIEL: Our friend didn't want to put her name to this for fear of offending others. We believed her story needed to be told.

Confront your inner fears –
you can't grow until you do.

DO YOU DARE?

Do you dare to succeed in all that you do,
To set a clear course and follow it through,
To dream without limit, to see yourself there,
To map out your journey with detail and care?

Do you dare to take action, to take that first stride,
Which most people shy at, and then set aside,
To sometimes risk losing all that you've won,
And start out again with your eyes to the sun?

Do you dare to build friendships, to touch others' lives,
To nurture and cherish, to constantly strive,
Knowing that sometimes false words will be spoken,
And friendships you value will fade or be broken?

Do you dare to keep trying though sometimes it seems
That to try any harder will shatter your dreams?
Do you realise that often life's path takes a turn
That doesn't make sense – are you willing to learn?

My friends, it's so easy to give up and say:
'I'll do it tomorrow or some other day.'
But triumph belongs to those who will dare,
To dream and take action, to risk and to share.

Michael Harrison

No pain, no gain.

CONFRONTING AND OVERCOMING

My son Greg had recently been to a Discovery Camp which focuses on improving self-esteem for teenagers. He came back with all the enthusiasm in the world to get out and do things in his life. One of these was to follow through on a long-held dream of doing a parachute jump. He approached me to drive him to the jump site the next weekend. Not enamoured with breaking into my own weekend, I asked how long it would take to drive there and back. Sensing my reluctance, he jokingly said, 'Well, if you don't want to drive backwards and forwards you could always stay and jump with me.'

I stared at him, horrified. 'Not this little black duck,' I said. I remembered how heights on lookouts always sent me rapidly backing away from the edge. Then a thought struck me. What was it I had always told my children? Wasn't it to face your fears? Here was my youngest son challenging me to practise what I preached, and I was backing down. After several days of agonising I decided to jump with him.

The weekend dawned clear and bright and we set off early in the morning. The training was to involve all day Saturday and half of Sunday and the jump was to be performed on the Sunday afternoon. As we registered, the young lady at the desk pointed at Greg and said, 'You can't jump, you are not old enough. You sounded much older on the phone.' Oh, what a dilemma. What was I to do? I was still booked in but it was Greg who really wanted to do the jump. Again I looked at the principles that I wanted him to live by and I realised that there was no reason why I should not go ahead. While Greg would of course be disappointed, disappointment is a part of life and something we all have to learn to handle some time. I remembered how my parents had overprotected me in my youth and how hard I had found disappointment to handle when I finally had to face it later in life. I put him on the train home and I stayed to do the training.

The jump was one of the most confronting things that I have ever done and I was absolutely petrified as I waited on the edge of the plane. The falling sensation, though, was fantastic, and I will always remember the feeling of utter stillness that came just after the chute opened and I was floating gently down.

However, my story does not end there. Two weeks after my jump I faced yet another confronting situation. Some months previously, after returning from living overseas, I found that the laws had changed and I could apply for my original birth certificate. You see, I was adopted. My friends and family could not believe how calmly I handled driving to the country town of my birth to search for any relatives. I found three sisters with my birth name still living in the town and I drove to the house of the one I was told would be home during the day. I knocked on the door and a huge man answered. I asked for Joy and was told to wait. He went back into the house and I heard him say, 'Joy, there is someone at the door for you. Don't buy anything.'

Soon I was peering through the flywire door at a small lady some years older than myself. Her eyes widened in recognition as she pushed the door open and I said, 'I have reason to believe that I may be your sister.'

'You certainly are,' she said. 'We have been talking about you recently and wondering how to find you.' I went into the house and was soon hearing about the huge new family I had discovered. You see, I am the youngest of twelve children, with six sisters and five brothers. It was a fantastic day with phone calls to my other two sisters in the area and to Melbourne where many of the others live. That day I also found thirty-seven new nephews and nieces who I would meet over the next few months.

It was only some hours later, when the excitement hit me, that I burst into tears. You see, I had just sailed through what should have been one of the scariest situations of my whole life but because of the jump a fortnight earlier it had been easy. Now when I face problems (or a set of 'challenges', as I prefer to call them), I head for the biggest and hardest of them all, knowing that by over-coming that one I will find the courage to deal with them all.

Margaret Seedsman

A NOTE FROM MARGARET: You might like to know that I gave Greg a parachute jump for his twenty-first birthday present and he not only completed his jump but also invited his father to join him.

*Face your fears – you will grow in
strength, courage and confidence.*

Who Am I
Really?

As a young girl I dreamed about what my life would be like as an adult. Would it be the life of a princess? Would I get married and have a family of my own? Would I be a successful lawyer or doctor? My mother assured me, like all mothers did in those days, that I would meet a man, get married and live happily ever after. She told me this man would look after me, probably taking over where my father left off, and I wouldn't have to worry too much about providing for myself in the world. Like all good little girls I believed her. When I was eighteen I went off to university to become a school-teacher, and while I was there I met him, my prince charming.

It couldn't have been more perfect. Peter was everything a young woman could hope for: tall, blond, blue-eyed, intelligent, well spoken, foreign (Danish), and an officer in the Royal Australian Air Force. I was the envy of all my peers at uni and my friends from school. And, I was in love, or as in love as any eighteen-year-old who had never been in love could be.

We courted throughout my university days and after my first year of teaching we married. Being a military wife was fantastic. We travelled extensively throughout Australia, and our constant social life was always fun and exciting. And to add to all this, Peter was amazing. He did all the things my mother said he would. He provided for me, took care of all the finances, insurances and any other essentials that needed tending. Peter did such a good job and I trusted him so implicitly that I left it up to him totally.

We continued to have this fabulous lifestyle for ten years, six of which we were married. We lived in most cities in Australia and I continued to work part time as a teacher wherever we went.

In 1986 we moved into a new house in Baulkham Hills, New South Wales. I was working full time and Peter was a pilot. One evening, he told me that several of his buddies were meeting in town for a drink. I encouraged him to go and suggested he stay the night with one of the guys to avoid driving home after drinking. He agreed.

It was about quarter past nine when he left, and I was so tired I was already in bed. As he drove out of the driveway, I remember having some really unusual thoughts. I began to wonder what life would be like without Peter in it: what I would do, how I would cope. This must have been some kind of premonition because at 9.36 p.m. Peter was killed in a car accident not more than five minutes from where we lived. A freak accident, the police said, and they assured me he died quickly and without any pain. The word 'fatal' took a long time to register with me. I just couldn't believe I was alone in the world.

I don't need to elaborate on the feelings I felt or the grief I went through, but the dilemma I faced was perhaps the most daunting one I had ever confronted in my life. Who was Victoria Hansen and why was she here on this earth? What was her purpose?

The years ahead provided challenge and heartache, one after the other. I began a journey of self-discovery I never dreamed possible, and I learnt things about myself I never knew existed. Finally, after six years alone, I realised there was a purpose to Peter's death. Until then I'd kept wanting to know why. Why me? Why him? Why now? Then one day I just woke up and I knew. He died so I could live, I mean really live, like I'd never lived before.

There are no such things as coincidences; everything in life happens for a reason. Once I came to know this, my life began to make sense. Events occurred exactly when they should, every incident taught a lesson, people came in and out of my life just at the right moment and I began to take notice and see everything differently, as if it were part of a map for me to follow. The map is never-ending, there is no treasure at the end, only a journey, a fulfilling and exciting journey that leads us into another and another. And just when you think you have it all together, it begins again, because you never know it all and no one has all the answers, only all the questions.

Every day I ask more and more of the questions that, I'm sure, perplex most human beings at some stage of their lives, and every day I find more questions than answers. But one thing is for sure, I now know that no matter what I do, where I go, or what I become, none of these is as important as who I am, and though I miss him very much, I thank Peter with all my heart for giving me the opportunity to find out.

Victoria Hansen

*The greatest growth and personal development
can come from adversity.*

DON'T EVER TELL ME I CAN'T

Every Saturday afternoon at one o'clock the old man would stand by his front gate, puffing on an old pipe or smoking a Woodbine cigarette, waiting for the first sight of his grandson coming up the hill.

The little boy would race up and throw his arms around the old man's legs and get a great hug in return. Then they would disappear inside the house where the youngster would chatter away like a magpie. The old man would just listen and nod until his grandson ran out of breath. When the time was right the old man would gently take his grandson by the hand, sit him down and begin the teaching.

During those early years, the youngster learnt to tell the time even before he started school. They used the grandfather clock in the bedroom or the old man's fob watch. The boy learnt the alphabet and could count to 100 with ease. He could read children's stories and understood the value of money. Often, the two of them would pop down to the local shop to buy a few things. The old man would always give his grandson a few shillings before they went into the shop. It was then the youngster's responsibility to work out how much the bill came to and to make sure he collected the right amount of change. If he got it right without any help, he was allowed to keep the change. It wasn't long before the youngster always got it right and started to collect a sizeable nest egg.

But the one thing the little boy remembered most was a saying that would help steer him through much of his life: 'Don't let anyone tell you that you can't do something. You can do anything if you set your mind to it and want it enough!' Naturally, being so young, the first time he heard those words he took them literally, much to the disgust of his parents. Whenever they forbade him to do something, the little boy's head would lift, back would go his shoulders, chin out, fists clenched and he'd repeat what his grandad had told him.

He eventually got the message, painfully, that there were some things that little boys *couldn't* do. The next time his grandfather sat him down and repeated those words, the youngster understood exactly what he meant. He also came to understand the importance of this special gift of determination.

At the age of ten he was told that he would never be able to swim – he was deathly afraid of the water, having once almost drowned. Then he remembered his grandfather's words and went on to become an international champion.

When his teachers said his school grades weren't good enough and that he'd never amount to much, he remembered the words again and became the school captain.

Then came a fateful day when he awoke in hospital and was told that he'd never play soccer again or swim for his country. His Olympic dream was shattered. He was told that if he ever swam again it would be with great pain and difficulty, and that he'd walk with a pronounced limp for the rest of his life. As he sank deeper into despair, he kept hearing snatches of the doctor's patronising words: '. . . need to make a few changes . . . lead a fairly normal life . . .'

Life for him until then had been sport, sport and more sport. The Commonwealth Games, followed by the Olympics, followed by a professional soccer career. He was so far down that for once in his life he believed people when they told him 'You can't' or 'You won't be able to . . .'

He's not certain when it happened – there was no blinding flash of inspiration – he just very slowly began to get angry until one day the medical staff felt the full brunt of his frustration and anger. 'Don't ever tell me I can't!' he screamed. From that moment on he focused his whole being on proving he could. He was going to swim again. He was going to run again and play soccer again. He had a dream again. Everyone who came into contact with him was left in no doubt. 'I am going to race again. Don't ever tell me I can't.'

A year later he achieved his dream; he was back in competition swimming. Although he never swam for his country again, he did win swimming championships, and he swam for the Royal Air Force for a number of years. His professional soccer career was washed up, but he was always out there playing friendly matches wherever he was stationed in the RAF. He later took up indoor cricket and played in competition until his mid-forties.

He has never rid himself of pain in his knee or shoulder and still experiences some numbness in his arm, but no one tells him he can't. No one tells *me* I can't!

It's as if, over the years, my grandfather has been by my side, guiding me, picking me up whenever I fell flat on my face. Perhaps he visited me in hospital when I was asleep. Who knows? What I do know is that his teachings have been an integral part of my life. I thank God that I was fortunate enough to have known and been loved by that fine old gentleman.

Rob Wilson

*You can do anything if you
set your mind to it.*

My Guardian Angel

Ever since I can remember I have felt an arm around my shoulders, guiding me through life and its turmoils. Could it have been the guardian angel the nuns always talked about? No, it was my sister. She was a beautiful girl with strong healthy features and a presence larger than life itself. She grew to be independent, with a fierce attitude towards achieving her goals. Her love for her family and friends was enormous.

As children, teenagers and adults we were inseparable – sharing our thoughts, feelings, dreams and friends. My sister was my idol; she lived life to the fullest and no challenge was too large for her to tackle.

When she married the man of her dreams, three gorgeous children followed. I was bewildered with her full life. She attended charities, joined committees, school functions, sporting rounds and even played in the occasional tennis tournament. Her days were overloaded and her evenings were just as busy.

Preparing dinner for eight people every night and spending quality time with her children and family was her favourite pastime. She would tuck her children into bed and read stories or sing lullabies before telling them each how special they were.

My son adored his auntie, and she loved him like her own. I was a divorced working mum but she wouldn't hear of anyone else looking after him besides herself. She would say, 'Bring him home to me, not to strangers.' So, gratefully, I did. I would arrive at night to take him home and find a giggling, clean and happy baby.

Whenever I felt unhappy about a situation or just tired she would cheer me up with a hug and kiss and say, 'Sis, I love you. Make every day a happy one; life is meant for living – make the most of it!'

Then, in 1984, there was a dramatic change in my sister's health. She would wake at night with cramps in her abdomen and severe pains in her mouth. She was only thirty-seven years of age. I came home to find tears streaming down her distressed face – the first time I had ever seen my sister cry.

My heart went out to her and still bleeds now when I think of how scared she looked. She pleaded with her gynaecologist for a hysterectomy, convinced that her pains were caused by complications with the birth of her third child.

After surgery the pains were still with her so she sought the best specialists the medical profession had to offer. When she lost confidence in doctors, she turned to alternative medicine. She saw a total of sixty-eight doctors, dentists, gynaecologists, naturopaths, chiropractors and anyone else who would take an interest in her pain. She was grasping desperately for some answers to her illness, but never believed the diagnosis was depression.

During her sickness we became even closer. Even though she had moved interstate we would speak on the phone *every* day, sometimes three or four times a day. It seemed that these talks were her only relief – knowing that we loved her and believed in the reality of her physical pain and agony.

As time passed, we witnessed her drastic change from a loving person with a lust for life to a sad, unmotivated, negative person who just lay there looking up at the ceiling. Sometimes her discussions turned to 'ending it all one day'. I would beg her to stop talking 'nonsense' and remind her of her very words to me: 'Live every day to the fullest and be happy. Life is meant for living!'

Her husband decided to take her overseas to do some skiing in Aspen and some shopping in New York and Europe. He hoped it would take her mind off her pain and put a sparkle back in her eye. But it didn't. The only shopping my sister wanted to do was 'doctor shopping', so desperate was she to find someone to tell her that everything would be okay again.

She rang me every day from overseas. 'I just need to hear your voice and tell you how I feel,' she would say. I would reassure her of our love and support and wished so much that I could give her the feeling of security she had always given me.

In 1994, during a much needed holiday to Bali, my sister rang me. She told me she loved my son and me and was so sorry to have caused me so much anguish and heartache over the past ten years. I told her how much I loved her and was looking forward to seeing her in four days' time. It was to be our last phone call ever. I learnt five hours later that she took her own life.

My 'guardian angel' is still with me and I will feel her arms around me forever.

Terri Caller

Accept all your emotions,
even the negative ones,
to begin the healing process.

A Case of
Cultural Theft

I came to Australia from the Netherlands in 1958. The advice from
the authorities in both countries – subtly given but insistent – was
to assimilate as quickly as possible.

To a teenager anxious to conform, this did not fall on deaf
ears. I spoke English wherever I could and came down like a ton of
bricks on anyone speaking Dutch in the presence of someone who
couldn't understand it, even in the most innocent of situations. I
was an Australian now, and my Dutch background and culture were
no longer relevant.

I stopped short of changing my surname, but I did fiddle
with my given name, which is Johan. This was considered too foreign, too 'new Australian'. In the 1950s 'new Australian' was not a
desirable epithet. An acceptable abbreviation, even in Dutch, is
'Jo'. Although I had never been called that, I settled for it, only to
discover that everybody wrote it as 'Joe' and called me Joseph when

they wanted to be formal. (This, incidentally, is still a problem.)

It wasn't until many years later that I embarked on a campaign to change the spelling back to 'Jo'. This was eventually successful, even though I continue to get letters addressing me as 'Ms'! Later still, I reintroduced Johan (even on my business card), and I now use the two interchangeably, depending on the formality of the situation.

This business with my name was only one of the more tangible symptoms of a general cultural identity crisis. Having married a dinky-di Aussie and being in the process of bringing up several children, I had plenty to keep me occupied. Yet I felt a growing sense of disquiet.

In the mid-eighties I started to repair contacts with relatives back in the Netherlands – contacts neglected for nearly three decades. We also began some serious planning to make a trip back to Europe for me to get back in touch with my roots and for my wife to see with her own eyes the environment in which I grew up. However, a year before the trip, something happened that put the past thirty years into perspective and gave me a new resolve for the future.

It was 1988 when I first read the book *The Dutch in Australia*, written a year earlier by Dr Edward Duyker, and his chapters on postwar migration opened my eyes. He explains how the Dutch government carefully toed the Australian government's 'assimilationist' line. The policy of both governments at the time was to counsel people to 'fit in', and the sooner the better. In his conclusions, Dr Duyker states, in part:

> Although the Dutch Government encouraged thousands
> of Dutch citizens to quit their homeland and settle in

Australia, they did not seek to retain active cultural links with them. Rather they encouraged them to lose their 'Dutchness'. For some twenty-five years, many Dutch tried to fulfil this expectation, but ultimately found the processes spiritually numbing.

Words fail me in trying to describe how I felt when I read that paragraph. Lights went on, veils were lifted and in one instant my feelings were vindicated and all doubt resolved. I now know that in 1958 I fell for it 'hook, line and sinker'. But I also know that for the last ten years my 'Australian-ness' has been immeasurably richer for my being able to openly and joyfully acknowledge my Dutch heritage as a vital and undeniable part of it.

For twenty-five years the powers that be (in which, in all honesty, I must include myself) deprived me of part of what I am. And I tell you this here and now: nobody is going to steal any part of me ever again.

Johan Kruithof

Be proud of who you are
and what you believe in.

CHRYSALIS

When our doctor had signed the death certificate, 'cause of death – dementia', he put his arm around me with great kindness. It was the end of my husband Warwick's long and distressing illness of Parkinson's disease and dementia.

As I sat alone by the screened bed in the nursing home and touched Warwick's thin and cooling body I remembered our magical lives together. We had been two artists working separately, but bonded by our deep love and our dedication to our work.

I thought about the slow, contemplative pace of our lives, and our delight in each other's paintings, each so different. I thought about his fine mind – he had been an art historian and a greatly loved teacher. I thought about his gentleness and heroic patience during seven years of cruel illness, the last four spent in a nursing home.

With my heart breaking open, I watched them place his

body in a black plastic bag. I stood alone on the street outside the nursing home and watched, desolate, as they drove him away in a little van.

It was then that I experienced the darkness and hopelessness of depression. I was isolated from family and friends, and even counsellors and support groups could not comfort me. My health deteriorated. I became dissatisfied with my work and all creativity seemed to leave me. I had painter's block and faced a terrifying emptiness.

Very gradually I began to see the blackness as a necessary time of healing and change. A time when the old has ended but the new has not yet begun; a time of metamorphosis as, in the darkness in the chrysalis, the caterpillar changes from a crawling, leaf-chewing grub to an exquisite butterfly, capable of flight and drinking nectar. This vision supported me through two more years of grieving until, at last, I began to paint creatively again.

I feel that I have been changed profoundly by Warwick's death. In learning to face the emptiness and loss, I have gained compassion and understanding at a deeper level. In spite of all the pain and suffering, it has enriched my life and was an experience I would never have missed.

Mahgo Smith Armstrong

Give yourself time to grieve – only then
can you move forward.

TAKE ME
AS I AM

Looking at my photo albums brings back all sorts of memories. I see happy snaps of family and friends, all of them showing me as a healthy, happy person. As I turn the pages, so many thoughts come to mind: the occasions, the places, and what prompted me to write the captions that accompany the photos.

Photos of me as a ten-year-old bear the caption: 'Such a big girl for her age, I think she needs to go on a diet.' The pictures show a very pretty girl, well covered, not fat, but still twice the size of her classmates.

Later there's a photo of an attractive twenty-year-old in a swimming costume with the caption: 'Reached my goal – just lost two stone.' Great photos follow, each one showing a happy woman fighting the battle of the bulge.

As the pages turn I see other comments that tell a story: 'Thirty years of age. Me looking sensational after six months of living hell. It was the worst diet, but worth it.'

Somewhere in the next ten years of photos I find a neatly written page: 'This was taken on the first day after my week at the health farm. I guess I am a classic yo-yo dieter. The weight is back on again and everybody is telling me I have to lose weight. I hate the way fashion says we have to be a size 12 and we shouldn't have more than whatever the body fat ratio is meant to be. I think I'll have to eat lettuce for the rest of my life.'

They say life begins at forty, and the photos of my fortieth birthday party show a confident, beautifully groomed, smiling woman who sparkles with happiness. It was about this time, as I remember, that it occurred to me how contented I was with life. A happily married woman with a beautiful daughter, I still found time while running my own business to swim each morning, walk the family dog, enjoy life with my family and friends, and stay heavily involved in community and charity work.

I have now learnt to enjoy life to the fullest without letting society dictate my fashion choices. I now understand that body shape is *not* a fashion issue but a health one. Each day I acknowledge that I am a unique person who has many talents and special qualities, and to the world I say, 'Take me as I am!'

Phillipa Challis

Don't be afraid to be yourself –
you are unique and special
just the way you are.

TAKING ACTION

KNOWING YOURSELF

Use this Action Planner to turn the messages in this

chapter into reality in your life. Turn to pages xvi–xvii to

learn the six simple steps you need to know to make the

most of this Action Planner and to enhance your life.

ACTION STEP

Create a collage of photographs from your life.
Frame it and hang it in a prominent spot as a
reminder of who you are.

MY SPECIFIC ACTION STEP

....
....
....
....
....
....

ACTION STEP

Pick one activity you have never done and have always been
fearful of. Take the appropriate steps and DO IT! For example,
use a chainsaw, go for a parachute jump, take a white-water
rafting trip, ride a motorcycle, abseil off a cliff . . .

MY SPECIFIC ACTION STEP

....
....
....
....
....

ACTION STEP

Keep a journal for thirty days.
Write in it every day,
even if it's just one sentence.

MY SPECIFIC ACTION STEP

....

....

....

....

....

....

ACTION STEP

Sit down and list every single strength you have.
Review the list a week later and see if you can increase
the number of strengths you have written down.

MY SPECIFIC ACTION STEP

....

....

....

....

....

....

ACTION STEP

If you are facing a stressful situation, seek the assistance
of a trained professional (counsellor, psychologist) –
they will help you grow from your adversity.

MY SPECIFIC ACTION STEP

....

....

....

....

....

....

ACTION STEP

Try yoga, meditation, tai chi, Shiatsu or any other
eastern practice that aims to calm the mind and
recharge the spirit.

MY SPECIFIC ACTION STEP

....

....

....

....

....

....

ACTION STEP

Spend a day alone, doing exactly what you want to do.
Go shopping, or see a movie on your own. Get to know
yourself and learn to enjoy your own company.

MY SPECIFIC ACTION STEP

....

....

....

....

....

....

ACTION STEP

Consider the 'labels' you use to describe yourself. For example,
'I am a salesperson', 'I am a wife and mother'. Create new, more
precise descriptions, such as 'I am an adventure-seeker who loves
business' or 'I am a fun-loving person who likes to help others'.

MY SPECIFIC ACTION STEP

....

....

....

....

....

BELIEVING

. . . be gentle with yourself.
You are a child of the universe,
no less than the trees and the stars;
you have a right to be here,
and whether or not it is clear to you,
no doubt the universe is
unfolding as it should.

PUSHING
THE LIMITS

Lying on my back in a gutter, a trickle of blood gurgling in my throat and ears, I am experiencing a level of pain I've never felt before. This is serious, but who is going to help me? I've spent nearly a lifetime rescuing people as a professional lifeguard. Now it's time to do what I've told hundreds of others – relax. That's hard to do when you have sixteen snapped ribs, a crushed lung and feel yourself fading fast . . . then it dawns on me – the pain is gone. I am looking down at myself, surrounded by onlookers, and an ambulance is tearing to the rescue. I feel a peaceful, wholesome joy. No! A wilful determination overcomes me and I am ready to fight the reality of finality. Dying is not an option. There is too much else in my life I have yet to experience: my daughter Amy, on the threshold of her own life, my wife Liz . . . Suddenly, there is a jolt of pain. Beautiful! I am back. The ambulance officer has stabbed me in the chest with a one-way air-valve needle, releasing the pressure from beneath my ribs.

As I lay in intensive care for the next five days, I had time to reflect on other aspects of my life that had been 'pushed to the limits'. Lowering my three-year-old daughter Lisa, who had been tragically killed, into her resting place, became a reality once more. I had, however, accepted her death as part of life and beyond my control. It was pointless wondering 'if only . . .'. It had happened, just as my situation had 'happened'. There was no time to look back. The memory of the anguish of Lisa's death, linked with my own close encounter, made my attitude to many things more vibrant. I felt even more determined to work at achieving my goals.

Within four months of rehabilitation I had become the coaching director of Triathlon Victoria, had won the Victorian and South Australian Olympic Distance Triathlon Championships, gained selection in the Australian team for the world championships, had placed second in the Australian Ironman Championship and had established a solid coaching business in triathlon.

All was going well until I received the news that every parent dreads. My 24-year-old son had been hit by a truck in New South Wales and was comatose with serious brain damage. The next act in my life was about to begin. But, like most of the other changes in my life, I had unwittingly been preparing for such a trauma for many years. I'd had a lifetime of physical training and fifteen years of mental discipline in a monastery. However, nothing could have prepared me for the emotional torture of seeing someone I loved suffering, knowing that his talents and dreams would never be realised.

Since those dramatic early days, my son's life has been filled with struggle, pain and confusion. We have to work carefully to determine his future. Part of the work involves 'pushing the limits' in an effort to make things happen for him. In doing so, I am also straining to meet the many other day-to-day demands on my time. In the end, however, there is a satisfaction in realising that life has a richness about it that can only be enjoyed if you are prepared to accept its complexities in a simple way. Understanding this is the only way I can cope.

Reflecting on the traumas that have been woven into the structure of my life I often rejoice about the energy I have been able to give other people through my interest in sporting activities: coaching rugby, heading a lifeguard team, coaching basketball and my current commitment to coaching people of all ages and abilities in triathlon. There is nothing more satisfying for me than to see the smile on someone's face when they have completed a challenge they thought was beyond them. They have learnt the simple principle of 'pushing the limits'.

As I start out on another daily training routine preparing for my latest triathlon competition, I think about the privilege of being able to do this. I know what it's like not to be able to. I also know what it's like for other people not to be able to. The driving energy I have to draw, paint, train, coach and enjoy my family is derived from my willingness to accept what has been and to look positively to the future. Belief in my ability to tolerate pain and disappointment has given me the wonderful capacity to relish life and its extraordinary, simple joys.

Oscar Carlson

*Use tragedy to tap into
your deepest strength.*

YOUR POTENTIAL
IS ENDLESS

The voice on the other end of the telephone sounded unfamiliar, hesitant, unlike any I had heard before. 'Hello, Jann? My name is Perry Cross. [Pause] I'm a quadriplegic on life support [pause] and I'd like to register for your [pause] public speaking course.'

For a moment I was literally stuck for words. How could I even consider the possibility of him participating in one of my courses? Over the years I had received inquiries from people with varied careers and interesting reasons for wanting to improve their presentation skills. There were strippers, electricians and managing directors, yet none as unique as this young man.

I tried to form a picture of him in my mind, but found this difficult as I'd never met a quadriplegic, even during my career as a nurse, and certainly not one who required a respirator to breathe.

'I'm twenty years old and I broke my [pause] neck while playing a game of rugby. [Pause] Sport was everything to me and

I'd [pause] like public speaking to be my new sport.'

My initial doubts rapidly dissolved as we continued our conversation. Yes, he did understand that others in the course may find his appearance a little difficult, even frightening at first. However, Perry believed that he could participate fully and complete the weekly assignments over the six-week period. I found myself genuinely excited about working with him.

On the first night of the course Perry 'rolled' into the seminar room (in his motorised wheelchair)and into my life. He took to speaking like a duck to water, amazing us with his lack of self-pity and enormous determination. The six weeks flew. Each of us grew to admire, respect and care about this incredible young man.

It was April 1994 when Perry's life had changed so dramatically. He fell, as a result of a high tackle in a rugby game at Ballymore in Brisbane, and broke his neck. His survival is one of medicine's modern miracles. For three months he could not eat and it was six months before he could talk. After lengthy negotiations and devoted family support he was allowed home to the Gold Coast to live. He achieved this in the record time of eight months from the time of his accident! (Many quadriplegics never leave hospital, and to do so under eighteen months is a milestone.)

Upon completion of my course I was so in awe of Perry's drive and the power of his message that I offered to help him launch his professional speaking career. On 28 February 1996, only six months after commencing his new career, Perry shared the stage with invincible motivator Laurie Lawrence and sporting champions Guy Andrews and Reen Corbett. He made history as Australia's first quadriplegic professional speaker on life support.

The crowd of 500 gave Perry a standing ovation for his inspirational talk on overcoming the obstacles in life and valuing relationships. As the television cameras rolled I felt as proud as anyone could ever feel.

Perry is a natural at his new sport and, while it is not without difficulties and unforeseen challenges, I believe you will be seeing a lot of him in the years to come. In Perry's own words: 'Your potential is endless, whatever your situation.'

Jann Stuckey

*A strong, positive attitude can overcome
the biggest obstacles.*

HOPE

It is a joy to be able to write about some of my experiences over the past few years. You see, I actually did not expect to be alive to tell of them. But I am still here, so off I go.

In July 1989 I was diagnosed with breast cancer and underwent surgery – a mastectomy – followed by chemotherapy for six months. I had several lymph nodes under my arm that were affected with cancer cells and I knew I had less than a 50 per cent chance of survival. Now, nearly seven years later, I have known many women with less severe breast cancer who have not survived as long as I have – so, who knows?

Since the original surgery, I've had further surgery to remove two rather large lymph nodes from my chest wall – these blighters were also malignant. It is more than eighteen months since I was diagnosed with secondary breast cancer in the bones; quite a few spots showed up on the scans, but fortunately I am pain free. The only treatment for my present condition is a form of hormone therapy, which has put me into chemical menopause. Should I start to feel pain I can undergo radiotherapy to ease it, but I am told that this treatment will only be palliative and there is no cure for secondary breast cancer.

The worst night of my life, however, was during the time of my first surgery. My husband and the children were on their way to visit me in hospital when my husband had a car accident. My daughter Sarah was in grade two at school and was just about to celebrate her seventh birthday. I do not have the words to describe my feeling of helplessness as I was wheeled into the ward to find my darling daughter in an indescribable mess. I could not count the stitches: half Sarah's face was sutured, a major gash extending from her mouth to her eye. It is a miracle she did not lose that eye.

When I was told the news of the accident, I was recovering well from my own surgery but I was not strong enough to care for Sarah. The only way my doctor would let me visit her was in a wheelchair. The night I first saw her I had to be wheeled out of that ward away from Sarah's view while I broke down into a thousand pieces knowing that I could not stay with her and look after her until I had recovered myself. In fact, my surgeon would not discharge me from my hospital until Sarah was discharged from hers. With hindsight, I must say that this was the right decision, but at the time I was devastated.

Six and a half years and two lots of plastic surgery later, Sarah is looking wonderful. She will have more surgery this year. Every day it seems someone comments on how miraculous her recovery has been. There have been many people who have expressed how beautiful Sarah is, despite the remaining scars. I remember at the time thinking how unfair it was for Sarah to have to suffer so much and lose a mother as well. Who would be there to guide her through the rocky days of her early teens? Would her face improve enough for someone to ask her to the first school dance?

It seemed at this time that the only news I was ever destined to hear would be bad. My marriage was over and I had to contemplate life as a single mother with a life-threatening disease.

I attended a program run by Ian Gawler on positive thinking and general pro-life attitudes. I read every book on cancer that I could get my hands on – self-help books now line my shelves. I joined a volunteer group trained by the Anti-Cancer Council to support women newly diagnosed with breast cancer. It seemed that most of the women I spoke to had also been through their own dramas.

All of a sudden a couple of years had passed and I was now talking to others about survival – telling them that there is no such thing as false hope. You see, I now subscribe to the belief that if it is possible for one person to overcome their life and health problems then it is also possible for others to do the same. Not everyone will, of course. The statistical facts remain as a constant reminder that we can never take our time on this planet for granted. For the people who want to live by statistics, there are plenty available. But those who choose to hope can breathe deeply and fill whatever time they have left with joy. It is simply a matter of choice. I have made mine. I choose 'hope', and it feels wonderful.

Elizabeth Trimble

*It's the choices you make in life
that make the difference.*

Anyone Can Do It

I'm not quite sure when it all started . . . maybe it was when I smashed the front of my car without realising I was even close to another car, or when I nearly ripped the phone out of the wall and threw it at the window because I was having trouble concentrating, or perhaps it was because I was beginning to feel like a sleepwalker, unable to distinguish day from night. What I do remember is a sense of urgency: something had to be done!

I had a one-year-old demanding to be breast fed every two hours through the night, a four-year-old wanting more attention, postgraduate assignments to complete, a home to upkeep, work to attend to . . . oh, and did I mention a life to lead?

I remember wondering if anyone had noticed I was living in the twilight zone. Maybe not. Maybe they just thought I was rehearsing for *The Rocky Horror Show*. I also remember feeling a failure because I couldn't get the baby to sleep, especially when people told me they had their child sleeping through the night within the first month.

As an independent woman who likes to think of herself as capable and intelligent, I didn't feel anyone could assist me. I suppose I also thought that, somehow, things would magically right themselves if I could just last a few more weeks. Besides, I was sure other women had managed with the same demands, so why not me? I thought I could juggle everything with harmony and a sense of humour, like a family on TV.

In retrospect I look back and see someone who grossly underestimated the demands of managing a family, study, work and a need to be more than just alive. I was under the misapprehension that I could use that 'spare' time while having babies to study, update my skills for a career change and do some part-time work – *and* do it all in some semblance of order. I also allowed myself to be burdened with the idea that I was 'just a mother' and 'unproductive' because I was relying on someone else to pay the mortgage. Of course this affected my self-esteem. I found myself sleepless, unable to focus on my studies, unable to find time to go to the bathroom without children in tow, having conversations that were primarily child-oriented, struggling with the fear that I was postnatally depressed, and unable to understand why I was so incapable of hanging it all together.

I did not plan for the 'special nights' either, when I would just be settling down to the first of sixteen assignments and my oldest child would come down the corridor in a 360 degree spin of vomit with her sister in harmonious pursuit. After numerous repeat performances it would be too late start work (my ability to write coherently had faded to nothing anyway).

At times like these I had serious doubts about attaining my

goals, but then somehow I'd take hold of a fleeting moment – on a bus or in a supermarket – when my creativity had begun to flow again, and this would get me through. I would remember what I was trying to achieve and this would keep me moving forward.

Eventually, I finished my course, the breast-seeking baby learnt to enjoy cow's milk and sleep beyond two hours, and those job offers did start appearing on the horizon. But the progress was so painfully slow that I was only able to see it by looking back; there were many moments I thought I would not make it.

My story is about a personal achievement that may not appear to be a grand achievement in the scheme of things, but it is a story anyone can relate to who wants to effect change in their lives. If you feel things are beyond your control and you *live* that feeling, you perpetuate the belief that you are incapable of creating your own opportunities. Believing in yourself is of paramount importance. The decision to undertake postgraduate studies was part of a series of changes and private victories that helped me feel good about myself again. I felt I could reshape facets of my life by making changes to my working life. Yet after the glory of every personal achievement a new day dawns, initiating a new set of hurdles to grapple with . . . but what bliss as we move forward!

Olga Florenini

*You can effect change in your life if you
are willing to put in the effort.*

THE DESERT
OASIS

The red centre of Australia is beautiful, unique – there's nothing else like it in the world.

When I first saw the red centre I was a young, impressionable 23-year-old backpacker who was madly in love with a beautiful, blonde-haired, bronzed Australian girl. We travelled around Australia by bus, train and hitchhiking. It was an adventure, to say the least. Of all of our travels around Australia the place that made the biggest impact on me as a young man was our visit to Palm Valley. We had seen Ayers Rock, we'd seen the Olgas, we'd slept under the stars in the beautiful red desert, but we weren't really prepared for what we were about to see.

We climbed onto the four-wheel-drive bus and headed off into the red centre. It wasn't a long journey, but it was a rugged one, at least compared to the long straight roads we'd taken to reach Alice Springs. It was slow and very bumpy as we made our way through the terrain and emerged into a beautiful green oasis, Palm Valley.

I couldn't believe my eyes. In the heart of one of the biggest deserts on the driest continent in the world was a lush, almost tropical valley. Our guide explained that many of the palms are considered some of the oldest in the world and that this valley of palms has been here for thousands of years. We learnt that Palm Valley has a life-sustaining source of water. No matter what the conditions, no matter how dry or hot the red centre is, Palm Valley continues producing its life-sustaining water.

That afternoon as we bounced up the rocky path on our way back to Alice Springs I realised that there is a 'Palm Valley' inside each of us. No matter how rough, dry or harsh our exterior, within each of us is a beautiful green oasis of life-sustaining energy which never ever dries up. That spirit keeps us going every moment of our lives.

Bouncing back and forth in the back of that bus, I made a decision to believe in my Palm Valley and to know that I can always rely on my deepest inner strength.

Daniel Johnson

Remember to love yourself,
it's your life-sustaining force.

ROBERT'S STORY

Have you ever noticed when you are really down that if you take the focus off yourself for only a minute and look over your shoulder, you suddenly see someone who has more problems than you, who is not as lucky as you?

I found myself meeting a lot of children who were 'unlucky'. They didn't see themselves as unlucky – they just accepted what life had given them – but their parents did. So these children were put on an intensive home-treatment program, working eight hours per day, six days per week, month after month after month. As the administrator of the American organisation which runs this very specialised program, I was privileged to take these children and their parents to America.

One little boy who came on my first trip over was called Robert. Robert was legally blind, couldn't move, and it more or less seemed as if there was 'nobody home'. But his parents, Sue and

John, would not accept this for their son. They went to America, got a specialised program for Robert and couldn't wait to get back to Australia to start. Of course, since John had to work, this was mainly up to Sue, but she had a lot of wonderful friends who were waiting to set up and begin the program.

At first it was a bit difficult. Everybody really wanted to get started, but equipment had to be built: for instance, a steep slide to teach Robert's healthy brain cells what movement was all about. Then there were the monkey bars, to help him slowly become used to the weight of his own body, with each bar painted a different colour (ready for when he could recognise colour). The toilet had to become the 'dark room' where Robert did his eye exercises with a torch. And he also needed a 'patterning' table on which he would lie while people helped to teach his brain about movement. Because he was only little (from memory he was two years old) this took three people, one to move his head and the others to move an arm and a leg each. Of course, this is only a brief outline of the program; there was much more to it than that.

Robert's parents worked for at least two years – an unreasonable length of time for an unreasonable problem. But the improvement Robert was making was quite remarkable. The last time I saw Robert, he was reading, running, and generally misbehaving – Sue had a dynamo on her hands. Robert was still brain injured and hyperactive, which, in itself, is a handful; but what a change! Some people use terms like 'miracle cure', but from firsthand experience I know it was plain hard work by Sue, John and their volunteers, and, of course, by Robert himself.

It is interesting to reflect that of all the parents I took to America, not one was promised anything at all. It was not known how these brain-injured children would react since the brain is an area of the human body about which we understand so little.

I will never forget the time I arrived with one group in Oahu. The immigration people were very good to us and used to open a special section for us to go straight through. I asked the group of parents to go through immigration and up the escalator to customs. As the last of the parents went through immigration, I walked to the escalator and there were all the parents and their children waiting at the bottom. As tour leader I asked them to move up the escalator, but nothing happened. Then I moved to the front of the group to see what was happening. A mother with her six-year-old boy in her arms was just standing there. I asked her to move up. She didn't. Then I noticed the tears in her eyes as she said, 'Trudy, I'm scared. We've never been up an escalator!' This mother, her husband and son had just come off a 747 jet. What we will do for our children!

Trudy Lightfoot

Believe you can make a difference
and you will.

AN AMAZING
ACHIEVEMENT

A few years ago, I took a trip through central and northern Australia. My aim was to learn about the things Australians are supposed to be familiar with. I threw boomerangs, sampled damper under a starlit outback sky and talked with local stockmen. It gave me a taste of a life I had often read about but rarely visited. I experienced the vastness of the outback, trekked through gorges beneath sheer rock faces, listened to the eerie moans of the breeze, saw amazing Aboriginal rock carvings, canyons and clear skies. My most vivid memory, however, is of an unexpected encounter at a homestead just south of Alice Springs in Australia's hot centre.

I was enjoying a leisurely horse ride across the ochre-red earth with a few friends when Gary Glazbrook (the owner of the homestead) came screeching by on his three-wheel motorbike. He stopped to introduce himself and then, after ensuring that we were enjoying ourselves, rocketed out of sight. I was glad I had met him, but even happier that his bike had not scared our horses, which must have been used to the noise.

That night, when we gathered around a log fire to hear Gary talk about outback life, it was lucky there were no flies, because several mouths opened in astonishment when the owner arrived in his wheelchair. Gary, a former shearer, lost the use of his legs after a car accident, and only has partial use of his arms. This has not stopped him from personally supervising the station's activities with the aid of a modified bike, controlled with one hand. Hence the open mouths. You hardly expect to learn that a man tearing around on a motorbike is a quadriplegic.

He has a humorous approach to everything. When you meet Gary, you forget within minutes that he has such severe physical limitations (if you ever find out, that is) but when you leave, you do not forget him.

It makes you wonder. Why shouldn't we dismiss our worries as easily as some people dismiss their disabilities?

Leonard Ryzman

It's not the problem that's the problem,
it's our reaction to the problem
that's the problem.

An Inspiring
Friend

Russ was a married man in his late thirties. He was the company secretary of a listed company, a lecturer at a technical college, a state table-tennis player; he had a wife and two children whom he adored, and went with his family to church on Sundays. Russ was not only liked but respected by all who knew him professionally and personally.

In February one fatal year he was diagnosed as having terminal cancer and was told he would not see the following new year. I visited him as often as I could. As his condition grew worse and he lost weight, I asked him, 'Russ, how can you put up with this great adversity – the knowledge that you will die within months?'

His reply was, 'George, I am a very lucky person. I learnt many years ago that if you are given a lemon you should make lemonade.

'I know when I am going to die, so I have all this time to

117

make proper financial arrangements for my family. I can spend the remainder of my time helping my wife and children deal with life without me, but more importantly I have time to make peace with my maker. But you, you can get run over by a car or have an accident or a heart attack with no notice at all. I am much better off than you are.'

What a wonderful attitude! What a fantastic lesson for all to learn.

George Paul

You can transform adversity into advantage.

ANYWAY

People are unreasonable, illogical and self-centred.

. . . Love them anyway.

If you do good, people will accuse you of being selfish or having ulterior motives.

. . . Do good anyway.

If you are successful, you will win false friends and true enemies.

. . . Succeed anyway.

Honesty and frankness make you vulnerable.

. . . Be honest anyway.

The good you do today will be forgotten tomorrow.

. . . Do good anyway.

The biggest people with the biggest ideas will be shot down by the smallest people with the smallest brains.

. . . Think big anyway.

People favour underdogs but follow only top dogs.

. . . Fight for some underdogs anyway.

What you spend years building may be destroyed overnight.

. . . Build anyway.

Give the world the best you've got and you get kicked in the teeth.

. . . Give the world your best anyway.

You see it's not the score that somebody else keeps on your life that counts in the end, it's the score you keep on your life that makes the difference.

Author unknown

Submitted by **Kevin Egan**

Have faith in your values.

BURNING
AMBITION

Way back in the days when yours truly was a fresh-faced youth I
had a burning ambition to be an artist. You could scarcely blame
me as I had just spent 'the best days of my life' (as I was frequently
reminded) convincing my teachers at St Virgil's College in Hobart
that I was no good at anything but drawing.

Anyway, here I was, leaving school in the year 1945, with
the world (what was left of it) at my feet and determined to earn a
living at what I knew best – drawing! It didn't take long for me to
learn that to qualify as a professional artist – I preferred landscape
in watercolours – it was necessary to live in abject poverty.

So I got a job in the state public service. Still wanting to
follow my chosen career, I began to attend evening art classes at
the Hobart Technical College.

It was here that destiny stepped in. I met a fellow Old Vir-
gilian – Christopher Koch – who had left school a couple of years

after me and who was now employed as an apprentice press artist at the local newspaper *The Mercury*. Chris informed me that he was about to abandon his career in newspapers and take off on the big overseas trip. I thought that if I applied for his job I could perhaps realise my ambition to be an artist and get paid for it.

The rest is history – I applied for the job and got it. At *The Mercury* I was extremely lucky to find myself under the guidance of the head artist, Norman Southey, who was a very talented cartoonist. I blame Norm for first planting the desire to be a cartoonist in my mind. He ensured that I would be utterly incurable by his enthusiasm in teaching me all the tricks of his trade. It wasn't long before I wanted to be a full-time cartoonist and, as *The Mercury* wasn't big enough for the two of us, I moved to the *Sun News Pictorial* in 1964. It was then that I finally realised my ambition.

It's interesting to note that Chris Koch, having had the courage to dump his job in favour of the unknown, has become one of this country's best known authors. One of his books, *The Year of Living Dangerously*, was later made into a film of the same name!

As for me, thanks to Christopher Koch and Norman Southey and my very patient wife, Pauline. I've had a marvellous time travelling the world, cartooning and just plain drawing. In short, being paid to do what I love best!

Jeff Hook

Nurture your goals and be open
to all opportunities.

I Had a Dream

The other night, I dreamed I was writing this piece on dreams. I didn't realise it was a dream at the time, although I should have suspected it wasn't real when my driving was never interrupted by a red light.

Science says we all dream. When people claim they never have, it's just that they don't remember their dreams. This leads me to speculate on whether some insomniacs believe they haven't slept only because they spent most of the night dreaming they were awake. Some people dream the winning lottery numbers, but I have more important things on my agenda. Last week I dreamed that Australians appointed an unknown plumber as Treasurer, because someone had to do something about all the money going down the drain. (I said important, not sensible.)

But some dreams are worth talking about, whether they sound sensible or not. One evening, I was looking at a beautiful full moon with a few people. One of them, Jim, said, 'When I was only ten, I looked up there and declared, "One day, I will walk on the moon!"' He was just like so many other people who reminisce about childhood dreams, except for two extraordinary differences.

Firstly, when Jim conceived his dream of travelling to a new frontier and walking on the moon, there was no such thing as space travel, let alone moon landings. That is why, as an adult, he had to settle for the next best thing – the goal of becoming a test pilot who flew the world's fastest planes. But despite this new goal, he was not deterred from his boyhood dream. It was just the best thing to do until technology caught up with his vision.

The second interesting thing about Jim was that he hadn't been disheartened by the laughter of family and friends when, as a boy, he revealed his dream. He was not even deterred by a plane crash that had him in hospital for two years, with nearly every bone broken. During that time, astronaut travel became a reality, but doctors ruled out his ever flying again, let alone becoming an astronaut – the elite of pilots.

If Jim hadn't nurtured his dreams while in hospital, he might not have walked properly again. So as we looked up at the moon, it was amazing to think that he was the seventh man to walk there. James Benson Irwin, the Apollo 15 lunar module pilot, was one of only a handful of people who had stood up there and looked back at our planet.

Jim said that before take-off, when mission control asked if they were ready, he had to laugh. He had been ready for that moment since he was ten. He had dreamed a big dream and didn't let go while working towards it, no matter how unlikely it might have seemed to others.

My meeting with that inspiring man remains firmly etched

in my memory. Now, if I could only remember how my dream about writing this piece on dreams ended. But more importantly for you, how will your dream end? You do have at least one, don't you?

Leonard Ryzman

Take especially good care of your dreams.
They are an important asset.

NEVER GIVE UP
ON YOUR KIDS

My son and I attend Little Athletics together. He competes, and I'm a dad who helps out. It's our father–son quality time and we love it. His mother, for some reason, does not complain about having an entire morning to herself.

I remember at the end of our very first Saturday morning at Little Aths, we got back into the car and I noticed my son was rather quiet.

'Did you have fun, son?'

'Dad, I didn't win anything.'

'Jono, it was your first morning. The others built up their experience last season.'

'Dad, I came last in *everything*.'

'No, son. You came eighth. We don't have last or second-last at Little Aths. We have seventh and we have eighth, but no last. Besides, next week you might get a seventh.'

And the next week he did get a seventh. But he went right through that first season without a win, and I knew that deep down he would have liked at least one win.

The second season came and went, and then the third season, and we had fun, lots of fun, but he still didn't win. Then in the fourth season one of the dads telephoned. They were a boy short for the zone championships the next Sunday. Jono put the phone down, his eyes sparkling.

'How many events are you in, son?' I asked.

'Just one, Dad, the 1500-metre walk.'

Now, I knew this wasn't Jono's best event. He had developed a style designed to avoid disqualification but as a result he was more often than not disqualified.

'Son, that's your worst event.'

He shouted, 'Dad, it's the zone championships!'

The next Sunday morning found us at the zone athletics stadium. 'Look, Dad,' he breathed, 'it's a real athletics track.' We knelt down to touch the genuine all-weather surface and the white lines that were painted on with real paint. He was so excited that he just knew he was going to go brilliantly.

And he did. The judges let him finish, but as he crossed the finish line, he walked three more steps and with a big grin broke into a jog. That's when the judges disqualified him. The rules say you must walk, not run, at least five steps after you cross the finish line.

He came over and sat quietly beside me on the grassy spectator embankment and I really felt for him. There are moments when fathers feel deeply, and I just ached.

The gun went for the next age group, and that race had two superb walkers in it. I said to Jono, 'Could you walk like that?'

and he said, 'I suppose so.' So we went over the back of the embankment and we practised both then and all week.

The next weekend we were back at our home track, and it so happened that the 1500 metre walk was on the program. The race started and young Jono took off like a rocket, walking like an Olympic athlete. A couple of hundred metres down the track he was already leading by 20 metres and I thought, 'Oh no! You'll never keep that up!'

His action was superb and even the judges were smiling. He was 90 metres ahead of the second-place-getter as he came to the finish line. He didn't smile, he didn't punch the air, he simply walked five extra steps. His time for the 1500-metres was 45 seconds faster than he had ever walked the 1100 metres.

A few minutes later I realised he was standing by my side.

I put my arm around his shoulders and said, 'I'm proud of you, son.' And for just a split second, my ten-year-old son, in public, hugged his dad.

Never give up on your kids. Their greatest surprises are still to come.

Malcolm Gray

Strive to achieve your personal best
and be proud that you have
the strength and determination
to keep trying.

My Story

When I was just a very young girl,
I had a dream to change the world.
Instead I became a teenage mum,
Changing nappies, wiping bums.
Three children later and I was sold,
I'll stay at home, my dream on hold.
Sixteen happy years seemed to fly,
The children grew and passed me by.

I hadn't even thought of it,
When opportunity knocked and gave me a hit.
My husband uttered these immortal words:
'Spread your wings just like a bird,
I'll support you all the way.
It's your turn now, I have to say.'

And so began my new career
In hospitality and cheer.

I started in a small hotel,
So small you couldn't even yell,
But like a sponge, I absorbed and grew.
I became a duty manager too.
And then the biggest shock of all,
A big hotel chain knocked on my wall.
They said, 'Come see a different view.
Sales manager is what we'll offer you.'

In Alice Springs is where I'd begun,
Eight years ago this career of fun.
And since then along the way,
I've grown and changed day by day.
My marriage has survived, it's true,
With laughter, love and even a blue.
For our vows we had to renegotiate,
Before we reached this happy state.

From Alice to Darwin and then to Perth,
Followed by Melbourne, for what it's worth.
And along the way I climbed the stairs,
Smashed the ceiling (and the chairs)
To get to where I am today,
In the thick of the corporate fray.
Partner marketing, based in Sydney,
For Asia Pacific – the job for me!

But stopping here is not my style,
Although it may be for a while.
I've come so far and loved it all,
Changed some things and had a ball.
The dream I had so long ago
Is mine to watch and be and grow.
For in whatever place you have to start
Belief in yourself comes from the heart.

Anne Massey

*Hold on to your vision for the future
and you'll be ready to soar
when the time is right.*

FROM A SHUFFLE
TO BEACH CRICKET

Life seemed settled for my parents after they moved to a small fishing village about an hour and a half out of Melbourne. It wasn't too far to make regular trips back and forth to see their family – their two daughters, their grandchildren and Dad's 97-year-old mother – and they were content in their new environment.

Dad's vegie garden was his pride and joy and it meant a plentiful supply of fresh vegetables to family and friends. He also bought a fishing boat, which kept him so busy I was able to take a trip to Europe with Mum. My parents hadn't been to Europe before and as much as Dad would have loved to go, his responsibility to his ageing mother kept him home. I tell you all this because life changes so quickly at times, we should take every opportunity that comes our way.

I came back after two weeks and left my mum to travel for several weeks on a tour.

A week after her return, our lives changed forever. My father went off one morning to move his boat to dry dock. He made Mum a cup of tea before he left and said, 'I'll see you at lunch time.' She never saw him alive again.

My mother had spent all her adult life with my father and was suddenly on her own. She struggled to come to terms with what fate had handed her and to take responsibility for her own life. Then, just weeks after my dad died, his mother also passed away.

In hindsight (an all-too-easy view) maybe things could have been handled differently, but it was the nineties and we tend to deal with things as quickly and efficiently as possible because that's all we have time for. It is hard to imagine the sheer loneliness and loss of self that occurs for someone losing a life partner in their seventies. My mother decided to sell Dad's boat and all his tools and fishing gear and to move back to Melbourne. It was so traumatic for her – even more so as she adjusted to living with my family and tried to make decisions for her future. I guess it was some kind of cold comfort for her having the financial security to make such decisions, but even that was taken away from her.

One morning while reading the Sunday papers, we discovered that Mum's accountant had been arrested for defrauding millions of dollars from his clients. Like my mother, they were all older people who had entrusted him with their savings, and he had repaid them by cheating them out of their security.

So the slide began. Unable to come to terms with it all – with the complicated legalities, the powerlessness, the feelings of fear and hopelessness – my mother fell deeper and deeper into a black hole of despair. Our family became divided and my mother had a nervous breakdown. I cannot tell you how pained I felt seeing my mother suffer so much – the electric shock treatment seemed so barbaric for the nineties. In the psychiatric hospital, one day blurred into the next and she remained in a kind of cocoon where no one could reach her. I watched my best friend, my mother, fade to a shadow of her former self. It felt so strange to take on a parenting role with Mum after all these years as her daughter.

But love and support and the will to live can overcome any tragedy, even for people in their declining years, and my mother did become well again. The introduction of a new member to the family, Alistair, who came with no history or preconceived remedies, helped take her from the brink of what appeared to be no return to igniting an enormous boost of confidence in her own ability to participate in life with her loved ones. In fact, she has just returned from an overseas trip with my sister, playing beach cricket at Anglesea with her grandchildren.

Against all the odds my mother has rediscovered the joy in her life, and can now look to the future.

Sue Calwell

*Always look for that glimmer of life
then nurture it and watch it blossom again.*

TAKING ACTION

BELIEVING

Use this Action Planner to turn the messages in this

chapter into reality in your life. Turn to pages xvi–xvii to

learn the six simple steps you need to know to make the

most of this Action Planner and to enhance your life.

ACTION STEP

Find a place of peace and solitude and spend thirty minutes brainstorming anything and everything you would like in your life. Review the list and decide which dreams you are willing to put in the effort to turn into reality.

MY SPECIFIC ACTION STEP

....

....

....

....

....

ACTION STEP

Recall a time in your life when you pushed yourself to a new level of achievement. For example, winning a race, excelling academically, learning a challenging skill. Enjoy the memory. Perhaps write it in your diary.

MY SPECIFIC ACTION STEP

....

....

....

....

....

ACTION STEP

Start every day with your own affirmation – 'I love life' or 'It's great to be alive' or 'Today is another glorious opportunity to serve others'. Repeat your affirmation to yourself five times before you even roll out of bed.

MY SPECIFIC ACTION STEP

....

....

....

....

....

ACTION STEP

Take a class in a subject you're interested in
but have never believed you
would be good at.

MY SPECIFIC ACTION STEP

....

....

....

....

....

ACTION STEP

Select a specific fitness event and enter it. For example, a marathon, a fun run, a triathlon. Develop an exercise program to prepare yourself for the event. It's often fun to enrol with a friend or family member for encouragement and support.

MY SPECIFIC ACTION STEP

....

....

....

....

....

ACTION STEP

Ask your partner to tell you why they chose to be with you. Later, write down what they told you in your journal.

MY SPECIFIC ACTION STEP

....

....

....

....

....

....

GIVING OF YOURSELF

As far as possible, without surrender,
be on good terms with all persons.
Speak your truth quietly and clearly
and listen to others,
even the dull and ignorant;
they too have their story.

THANK YOU,
MISS...

I am not one for dropping names (apart from other people's), but I'm sure she won't mind. One night – which, let history record, was Thursday 10 September 1987 – I had dinner with Meryl Streep. She may also recall having dinner with me; but I shall never forget having dinner with her. It was – oh, it was just *wonderful*.

Ms Streep was in Melbourne to play Lindy Chamberlain in the film *Evil Angels*. However, once I survived the surly security guards and got over the threshold, as you can imagine, the evil evaporated and it was angels all the way.

I started by saying . . . no, actually, I started by *looking* for about half an hour. When my mouth was working again, I said that I made my living giving speeches as different characters. Ms Streep very politely replied that she did pretty much the same thing. I smiled. She smiled. I thought, 'We've got so much in common.'

All jesting aside, it was without any doubt the evening of a lifetime. I felt like the only other person in the room. As I was about to leave (on a passing cloud), she briefly put her hand on my shoulder (prefiguring the heart-stopping gesture she was to use with Clint Eastwood in *The Bridges of Madison County*) and said, 'Thanks for helping make my stay in Melbourne so much fun.' She smiled. I smiled. And before I could think of a parting remark . . . *I woke up!*

Alas, it was only a dream – just the kind Meryl Streep regularly weaves for us on the silver screen. But now let me tell you a true story, about real love. How many of us can't think of one teacher who's made a difference to the person we've become? For a few weeks in grade six at Camberwell Primary School, we had a student teacher called Miss Westh. I fell in love with her. Unfortunately, she already had a boyfriend. But fortunately, she saw in eleven-year-old me a spark of something – the incipient class clown, I suspect – and one night she took me to see the great French mime artist Marcel Marceau. And I fell in love with the theatre. Over three decades, through the vicissitudes of both our lives, we've managed to keep in touch. And a few years ago, when my own son was nearing the age that I had been in 1963, I took Pamela to see Marcel Marceau. As the lights went down, with my second wife on one side and Pamela and another dearly beloved friend on the other, I thought (unoriginally but with feeling), 'It doesn't get any better than this.' I shall always believe that you can never completely repay the debt you owe to someone who does something magical for you when you're young. If my life stands for anything beyond the ephemeral characters I inhabit, it is, I hope, as an essay in friendship.

In 1996, Camberwell Primary School held a fundraising

evening. Pamela was there. My speech was entitled, 'Thank you, Miss Westh: Recollections of a Class Clown Who Never Grew Up'.

And I hope I never do. Thank you indeed, Miss Westh. And good night, Meryl.

Campbell McComas

A NOTE FROM CAMPBELL: This contribution was partly based on a news commentary in 1987 for ABC Radio.

True friendship is a lifelong endeavour.

A Story about Christmas

Each year I find some aspects about the time leading up to Christmas somewhat disturbing. The unrelenting pressures of unreality and triviality hem me in. I am greeted by people who are either in a state of mental exhaustion or alcoholic hangover.

On one of the few occasions when we have a mandate to extend a little peace on earth and goodwill towards others, we cannot find the time or the physical strength to do either because we are using up both by rushing into ever-narrowing circles getting nowhere.

Even the pleasure of giving is diminished because the awesome, ever-growing lengths of artificially extended shopping lists preclude a leisurely and thoughtful approach to the act of kindness. Even the Christmas party is rarely enjoyed because so many trifling tasks remain undone and we cannot relax.

Have we made Christmas into something which is exactly the opposite of what it should be?

I wonder if it is appropriate that the birthday of the most beautiful human being ever born should be celebrated by drunken sprees, overeating and the pathetic groping that inevitably occurs halfway into the office party. Where there should be calm, there is clamour; gluttony replaces compassion for the starving; where peace should be enjoyed, we become white-knuckled with tension.

The pomposity, wealth and frigid detachment of many Christian churches contradict the simplicity and humbleness of Bethlehem. The atmosphere of the sparse, smelly stable does not, in reality, transpose into the grandiose and hideously expensive surroundings of an incense-burning cathedral.

Most Christmas functions are strange birthday parties because the guest of honour is never present – he is not even missed!

Last year we went to a different Christmas celebration. There was no doubt that the guest of honour was there that day.

The Variety Club is a group of show-business people and other celebrities who do an awe-inspiring job of raising heaps of money to buy amenities for physically and intellectually handicapped children. It was the club's annual Christmas party for them. There were over 1500 of them there, all with their loving parents and minders.

The smile of the guest of honour was reflected on the faces of the parents who watched; people who had gone through a hundred private hells, about which only they and God would know. Then there was the incident as we departed. It reaffirmed that the unique young man who tried to teach us compassion, love, forgiveness and respect for the poor and the weak was around that day.

A fat ugly man was leaning on a shovel outside the building while doing some repair work. We had seen him there several times before and had always noted his foul temper and nasty attitude towards everyone – particularly children. He had been his usual nasty self earlier in the day when we had entered the building. His heavy frame and ample gut would quiver with laughter as some child met with some discomfort.

I saw him being approached by a tiny beautiful girl – aged about eight – who propelled her twisted and emaciated body towards him in her wheelchair. She held out a toy wooden truck she had been given by Santa Claus. From her prostrate position she said, 'Please take this. I'm sure you know a little child who would like it. I already have plenty of toys at the home.'

The surge which came into my chest and my throat made me turn away. I looked over my shoulder and the man's back was towards me. His shoulders were shaking – heavily, helplessly – but not from laughter.

The Honourable Don Chipp

Genuine giving profoundly impacts others.

THE
COMPASSIONATE
POSTIE

After the football one sunny Saturday afternoon I was walking through Paddington with a friend when he stopped in front of a beautiful terrace house and told me that, six months ago, the house had been owned by an old lady in her nineties.

At that time the postman, who had recently been assigned to the area, was walking by, and noticed the little old lady coming out of her house. He saw her struggling up the front path with her four-stick walker to collect her mail. She took one painful shuffle after another. Over the next month the postman noticed the old lady a few times and saw what an effort it was for her to do the simple task of collecting her mail. He figured it must have taken her up to twenty minutes to get from her front door to her letterbox and back; she needed to stop every few steps to rest.

One weekend the postman visited the local hardware store and purchased a brass letter-deposit slot. He then drove over to the old lady's house, knocked on the door and waited patiently. When she finally opened the door, he politely asked if she would mind allowing him to install the letter deposit slot in her front door to save her walking all the way to the letterbox every day. She agreed. So he installed it then and there for her.

For the next few months when he delivered her mail he would walk up to the front door and push her letters through the slot. He never came across the old lady again.

One day when he turned to walk up her path, there was a man waiting on the front step. He introduced himself as the old lady's solicitor. He informed the postman that the old lady had died and asked if he could redirect all her mail to his office. He asked the postman his name and how long he had been the postman in that area. He then handed the postman an envelope which contained a letter from the old lady. It read:

> You, Mr Postman, showed me more kindness than I have
> ever received from even my own family. It's been twenty
> years since I have heard from them. They would not go
> out of their way for me, but you did.
> God bless you for the rest of your life.

She had left her house, furniture, belongings and early model Cortina to the postman.

Brad Cooper

Never underestimate the power of a kind deed.

BEYOND
EXPECTATIONS

Let me take you back to 1963 and tell you a story that will give you some food for thought. It was New Year's Eve and my father was riding his motorbike home from work when suddenly he was hit by a car and killed. I was six years old. My mother was left to bring four children up, alone. Not until some years later did I get over the loss of my father.

I didn't have much confidence. I didn't feel very intelligent. I felt different from the other boys. I was shy. I felt I was lacking in strength. And I believed that this was just the way I was. It wasn't.

I took up karate, and my instructor, Vince, took the time to show me the bigger picture. He was my first mentor. Later on I took a position on staff in a sheltered workshop and there I realised we can all be a lot bigger than we think we are, or are told we are.

I met Maria. She had cerebral palsy, and could not speak in

the way that we speak. She had to mumble her words and could not feed herself. She completed a Bachelor of Arts. Yes, a Bachelor of Arts.

Then there was Max, who could not move his arms and legs but worked all day stripping film with his mouth. And Robbie. Robbie's job was to move things. He could not use his hands and legs properly so he had a head brace and attached to that was a stick and he would push the work along with his head. Robbie did not stop. What he was born with did not stop him from being who he wanted to be.

About that time, I was teaching karate part time and Philip wanted to come along. He would wheel his wheelchair in the rain to get to the classes and during the classes he would get down on his knuckles and do push-ups while I held his thin legs. He would push and push and you could hear his groans as he pushed, and he pushed harder than everyone else in the class. And you could feel how this man would go far beyond the limits of what he was born with. What an inspiration.

I was working in the carpark of a major corporation in Melbourne and I joined Toastmasters. I told the human resources people and the executives that I was doing Toastmasters and they said, 'Steve, would you like to go on a self-development course?' I took the opportunity. After I completed the self-development course they asked me if I would like to go on a facilitator's course and learn how to run these courses. I could not believe it; these people had gone out of their way to give me a chance and I was only working in the carpark.

My confidence has grown because of the help of these people. So, if you can be a mentor to someone and help them grow, they will help other people in turn, and so on. Nobody has to be stuck where they are, they can go on to be bigger and better. We can break those beliefs that are so ingrained in us.

Steve Humphries

Encourage initiative in others and delight in their growth.

COMMUNITY
SPIRIT

Many years ago when I was a young mother with two small sons, my husband and I went to live in a small country village in north-western New South Wales. The village was on a railway line and was an important wheat-receiving centre. At harvest time it came alive with convoys of trucks transporting wheat to the huge silos, but for the rest of the year life went on in a peaceful way. The town's main activities revolved around the two-teacher school, the local memorial hall and the sporting facilities.

Our house was a pleasant one with a nice garden, but the village itself was a mess, with old machinery lying around, masses of rubbish of all kinds and a general air of total neglect. This worried me for quite a while until I suddenly had the idea of organising a town clean-up. We notified everyone that it would begin on a particular Saturday morning and asked people to bring as many trucks and tractors as possible.

On the day, the thought crossed my mind that perhaps no one would come, but to my utter amazement the whole village turned up – men, women, children and dogs, together with assorted machinery.

We started at one end and as we moved through the village many truckloads of rubbish were taken to the dump. After a full day and a few hours on the Sunday everything was immaculate with not a stray bottle in sight.

From that day on we all seemed to have a much greater pride in our village and it did wonders for people's self-esteem. Now when I see the wonderful work done in the annual 'Clean Up Australia' campaign, my mind goes back to that very special day when a little community's spirit came to life.

Nanette Lilley

*Have the courage to act on your ideas
and anything is possible.*

NEW LIFE
IN HEAVEN

The first time I stepped out of a Qantas 747 jumbo jet, I thought I was in heaven. The city of Perth and the Swan River were so peaceful, clean and beautiful that I could not believe my eyes. I kept asking myself, 'Is this real or am I just dreaming?' That was in late March 1980, a few years after the Vietnam War, and after I'd spent eleven months at a refugee camp in Indonesia.

But soon after I arrived in Perth I faced many difficulties, including loneliness, homesickness and a foreign language. At the age of fourteen, I had only a pair of thongs, a few shirts, shorts and a pair of trousers (no shoes, socks or even jocks) and one word, 'okay', which I'd picked up from an American soldier.

At the time I left Vietnam my father was still in a concentration camp. The remainder of my family could not leave my father behind and they could not afford to leave Vietnam anyway. I had a free ride on one of the many tiny fishing boats.

A few months after I arrived in Australia, my parents, a younger brother and two younger sisters escaped Vietnam. Three months after they left Vietnam I had a letter from one of the four survivors of the group, saying that Thai pirates had killed my mother and two sisters. My father and brother survived but were taken away by the pirates. They are still missing somewhere in the 'killing sea', the South China Sea.

Suddenly, life in a strange country became even lonelier, particularly every time I heard the sound of the kookaburra in the garden of the hostel. However, my life had endless freedom and was very peaceful, maybe too peaceful, so that tears often impaired my courage. But even tears and loneliness had not erased my mother's last words to me before I left my home in Vietnam: 'You have the intelligence. I just wish you could finish your education, then I'll be happy.' I guess those last words motivated me to learn English then finish my Higher School Certificate, and somehow I found a way to complete a degree in mechanical engineering.

I hear that life in Vietnam is getting better, but it will take time to be as good as here in heaven. I hope one day I have an opportunity to make my contribution as an engineer in Vietnam as I have already been able to do in Australia. The memories of the Vietnam War may never be forgotten but the people are willing to make a contribution and I think this is crucial if Vietnam is to become a livable place on this earth.

Khanh Do

Encourage others to reach their full potential –
sometimes all it takes is a few inspired words.

WALLY REALLY
CARES

I never cared for Wally Lewis. He was one of the best known sport-ing names in 'sport crazy' Australia in the 1980s. The reason I didn't like him was simple. Each year, in the Rugby League State of Origin matches, he would lead his team of marauding maroons from Queensland and beat the daylights out of my New South Wales side. You know what it's like, it's hard to see really good players on the opposition side. But when Wally Lewis played for Australia against England . . . ah, well that was different. Then I loved him: the way he led the team; his long cut-out passes; the way he bamboozled the Poms – ah, it was a joy to behold.

But nine-year-old Matthew Devins, also from New South Wales, managed to put aside state prejudices. Wally Lewis was always his hero. To Matthew, Wally was the 'king' of Australian football. Matthew was dying of leukemia. The story of Matthew's illness had been related to Wally, so on a promotional tour to

Matthew's home town of Tamworth, Wally scheduled a visit.

Come with me a moment, in your imagination, and watch Matthew's eyes grow big as pies when he opens the front door of his home and sees his hero on his doorstep. Come with me again, a month later, when Wally invites Matthew to join the Lewis family at Dreamworld on Queensland's Gold Coast. Be there, in your imagination, watching Matthew and Wally's kids, Mitchell and Lincoln, speeding around the dodgem-car circuit. Hear Lincoln, when Matthew smashes into him, say, 'Give yourself an uppercut!' (A good Aussie colloquialism jokingly meaning 'You had better smarten up!')

Come with me again, soon after the Dreamworld experience, to the funeral of Matthew Devins. See Matthew, lying in the tiny coffin, wearing the number six football jersey worn by his hero Wally Lewis. See the coffin carrying the colours of the Queensland team.

During the last few days of his life, Matthew asked his dad to give a message to the Lewis brothers. He suggested Mitchell should keep practising on the computer and that Lincoln should 'Give himself an uppercut'.

Now, I don't know how much Wally Lewis knows, but I do know how much he cares, and that makes him very special in my eyes.

Max Hitchins

Make a positive impact on others –
show them how much you care.

A REAL HERO

I didn't believe in heroes until I met Lois Chelumbwa.

I met her when I was visiting World Vision projects in Africa. We travelled down to the southern part of Zambia to visit some of the remotest areas in Africa. We stopped at a house beside the main road and Lois bounded out the front door. She was dressed in her best clothes and made up as if she was meeting some dignitary. She had one of the most disarming smiles I have ever seen, yet it was clear that she would not hesitate to make her point understood.

A grandmother, Lois retired in the late eighties after a life-time of service as a registered nurse. Not long after her retirement she became aware of the suffering of the women and children of a nearby valley. So she decided to come out of retirement and give herself to helping them. Each month she spends twenty-one days travelling some of the worst roads imaginable – to travel a few kilometres may take several hours. She and a small team of nurses will spend the whole day immunising children, listening to the mothers explain their problems and giving whatever help they can. Lois and her team do not eat during the day, they eat in the late evening and often have to stay over in a village sleeping on hard mud floors.

She tells many stories of the suffering endured by the women and children of the valley. Stories such as the mother who gave birth to a three-month premature baby who weighed only 800 grams. She was too far from any medical facility, so the baby, the size of a large mouse, had to survive in bush conditions wrapped daily in fresh leaves. Today, despite all the odds, the baby is alive and well. Lois visits the mother and child every month to monitor the child's progress. 'He's my precious baby,' says Lois.

Another story she tells is of a mother in a very remote part of the valley who went into labour. After thirteen hours the child would not come out. Her husband put her on a wooden sledge and, using a bull for power, dragged his wife across rough bush terrain for several hours to a lake. Then they had to wait for an hour for a passing canoe to take them across for help. This took another few hours. Meanwhile the weight of the child became heavy in the womb. The child was dead but now the mother was facing death. She finally arrived at the remote health clinic where Lois was work-ing that day. When Lois saw the state of the mother she took quick action to stabilise her condition and then rushed her to a hospital, which was a further four hours away. The mother survived and is very grateful to Lois for saving her life.

Lois arranged to go to the village where the mother lived. It was in a very remote part of the valley. In fact, when the vehicle drove in, the children ran away because they had never seen a car before. Lois conducted a health survey of the area and found that the children had not been immunised. There was no health clinic or facility within easy walking distance.

Today she includes this village in her monthly tour of villages. Now most of the children under five years of age are immunised and the mothers, especially those who are pregnant, are checked regularly.

Lois took me to meet these women. We travelled in a four-wheel drive on paths and across creeks that would test human patience to its limit, bouncing and rocking from side to side on seats as hard as wood for up to six hours at a time. When we arrived at these villages, I could see how the women and children loved Lois so much and how Lois loved them back.

After one of these arduous treks through the bush, I asked Lois why she didn't just stay at home and enjoy her retirement, instead of spending hours being thrown about in a four-wheel drive. She replied, 'I love the women and children of the valley and I want to help them.'

What amazes me the most about Lois is that she is one of the happiest people I have ever met. She has a contagious laugh and an inexhaustible energy. Despite living a hard life, travelling on the roughest roads on this earth, and having to work in atrocious conditions, she wouldn't give it up for all the money in the world.

Lois has restored my belief in having heroes. Not only is she a hero to admire but, more importantly, an example to follow. The difference between Lois and the superheroes of my youth is that Lois is real. And what makes her a hero is that she puts others first.

Leo Orland

Loving and helping others generates joy and energy.

CHARLIE

One of the best things I have ever done was hold my friend Charlie's hand as he died.

Charlie was in his seventies and, after a lifetime of smoking, had already had one leg amputated about ten years earlier. He had an artificial leg made of fibreglass that started just below the knee. He used to go to AA meetings, where he would take the leg off and stand it in front of him (it must have been uncomfortable to wear all of the time). The first time anyone saw this they usually did a double-take and probably thought, 'Yuk! That's disgusting!', but, after a while, people got used to it.

Charlie did not have much in the way of material things. He had a room in a home run by the St Vincent de Paul Society and spent most of his time providing voluntary assistance at the local AA service office, talking to suffering alcoholics who would call on the phone for assistance. Charlie had a great way with these people and would try to put them in touch with others who they could relate to. If the caller was a marketing professional who lived in a well-to-do suburb, he would try to find another professional person from that area and then get the two together. He had a profound inner peace as the result of practising a spiritual way of life. He was not religious; he simply trusted in a 'higher power' to guide him through life. He believed that in order to keep what he had, he first had to give it away. He helped people and provided service to the community, and in return he obtained his own serenity. It was through association with people like Charlie that I learnt that it is what is inside that counts, not what is on the outside.

Some of us would have dinner at Roy's place on Tuesday nights. Charlie would be there and he would spit little bits of bread roll at you when he spoke, or he would sometimes dribble a bit and, occasionally, forget to do up his fly. Did we care about these things? Of course not. That was Charlie and we loved him.

When Charlie was admitted to hospital, my wife and I were away. We came back late the same night and visited him at half past two in the morning. He had already had his other leg amputated, but he was coherent, knew who we were and was very pleased to see us. Charlie was grey against the blue of the room and the bottom half of the bed was flat where his legs should have been. He could not carry on a long conversation but he knew that we cared for him. He inquired after our health and was comforted by the visit.

At seven o'clock the same morning I went back with Frank and Nick. But by this time, Charlie was not able to speak to us. As he drifted in and out of consciousness, he knew we were there but could not communicate beyond a squeeze of the hand. We stayed for a while and left at around nine o'clock to go to Nick's for coffee. Soon after, we received a call from the hospital that Charlie was dying.

His time came at 11.17 a.m. Frank, Nick and I were with him. Frank cradling his head, Nick and I each holding a hand and whispering to him. We watched the heart monitor next to the bed and saw as his heartbeat gradually slowed down, sped up, faltered a bit, slowed down and then sped up again. This cycle was repeated for a few minutes as his breathing became harsh and deep. Then Charlie's breathing slowed right down and his heartbeat gradually faded away. The line on the monitor stopped peaking, and became just that – a line.

Frank wept a little. I felt deeply privileged to have witnessed this moment, and felt certain I had sensed Charlie's spirit leave his body. I remember a feeling of great peace and serenity. It was a profound experience. I now say that if anyone has the opportunity to be with a friend or loved one when they die, do so. It is one of the greatest gifts we can give them.

Trevor Housley

One of life's greatest pleasures is giving.

HAPPY HOUR

Bangkok was spread out beneath our feet. The windows of the luxurious hotel lounge overlooked the city and, far below, the giant snaking course of the Chao Phraya River. We watched its turbid water, patterned with the surging wakes from the never-ending string of barges and passenger-packed ferries. We watched the long-tail boats crisscross the river traffic like frantic pond insects.

We sauntered across to the bar to select spicy Thai cocktail titbits and settled comfortably into a soft lounge, sipping our complimentary drinks. Conversation and refills flowed. Introductions were made with the family on the adjoining couch. The father, a doctor, made positive conversation, while his wife, neutral in dress and manner, sat with nervous fingers constantly pulling at each other, not joining the talk easily. Their daughter, slim and attractive, continuously tossed her long blonde hair and gestured freely. They were in Bangkok for a holiday week, before travelling up-country so the parents could see where their daughter worked.

Conversation was desultory, touching on Thai country life, individual experiences and general sights. The mother briefly joined in, looking happier as travel stories were exchanged, but she was still perched tensely, constantly turning her head to watch as her daughter with the smiling eyes replied to our questions. Our happy-hour talk carefully avoided politics, or 'that war' just outside the Thai border.

Then the girl produced a surprise. She was a medic at a border camp for Cambodian refugees. We looked at her with new eyes. The name of the camp was well known for the severity of guerilla raids it endured, and its heavy mortality rate.

Glasses were discreetly refilled, more savoury nibbles brought to tempt our appetites. Words continued to ripple and eddy past. Voices to the side of us discussed shares, sales and tourist traps. The daughter's talk became optimistic, of numbers healed, families reunited and supplies that must come in from outside to help her group save lives threatened by injury, torture and disaster. Cosily ensconced in that luxurious cocktail lounge, sipping well-chilled martinis, the struggles she spoke of were an unbelievable world away.

Her nails were chewed to the quick. Understandable, I thought. She had a habit of nervously biting them as she talked. The father absent-mindedly removed her hand from her mouth and patted it down onto her knee, with a quick shake of his head. It was an automatic correction for a child who must one day have the nails of a lady. Did he still see her as a six-year-old, a little girl with tidy plaits safe in Holland? The eyes of the mother became bleak as she watched and remembered. Puzzled at his gesture, the girl paused mid-sentence, a quick frown turning to a small smile of recognition of both the gesture and her distant childhood. She changed conversation to lighter aspects of border camp life and her mother relaxed.

As they left for a dinner cruise on the great river below, we said farewells. I took the hand of the mother and held it briefly. In that instant she looked at me with unguarded eyes of sheer misery, as if she were unable to consider a future beyond the safety of these hours with her daughter. She grasped her daughter's hand tightly and quietly hoped we would continue to have a pleasant journey. We wished her the same on her visit to that camp. In turn, we shook hands with the girl and wished her well. Our words were pitifully inadequate for the border camp and conditions to which she was returning, but they had to do. How otherwise could we end a happy hour?

Noëlle Tolley

*Move out of your comfort zone to help
those needier than you.*

THROW STARS

When I was seventeen and about to embark upon my first full-time job (a trainee manager in an upmarket delicatessen), one of my first challenges was finding something to wear! At the time, I was living with my grandmother, so she and I paid a visit to Waltons flagship store, on the corner of George and Park Streets in Sydney.

There we were on the fifth level, thumbing through rack after never-ending rack of male apparel. At this point in my life I had no idea about colour coordination, 'power dressing' or even dressing for success. The store attendant, a portly lady in her mid-forties, came up to my grandmother and me, a tape measure draped around her neck. She asked whether I was looking for something specific. My grandmother answered by explaining that I was start-ing my first full-time job as a trainee manager and needed some appropriate clothing. Without saying a word (and nor had I at this stage), the woman looked me up and down a couple of times. I wondered what was coming, her face gave nothing away: 'Hmmm,' she said. 'He looks like managerial material.'

Now, I don't know if this was a well-rehearsed line for a situation such as this one or not. But judging by her tone and her willingness to invest an hour with us to make sure the clothes fitted well and matched, I'd say that it came from the heart.

What she'd done was to throw me a star . . . 'He looks like managerial material.' From time to time her words would come back to me, most often when the chips were down and I was losing confidence, and it would be as if someone had turned on a light! Her simple words helped me to appreciate my own worth; to let me know that I was the kind of person who would learn from and give to my work, and to take what I had learnt with me through life.

What that Waltons lady did that day was give from the heart. She threw a star and I caught it. And it has been lighting my life ever since.

Steve Barker

Never miss an opportunity to build the
self-esteem of another person.

CHILDREN
WITH HOPE

My daughter, Caroline, is working in Bucharest, Romania.

Romania is a Gothic, brooding country – the home of Vlad the Impaler (Dracula), the mythical Carpathian Mountains and the province of Transylvania.

The people of Romania suffered horribly during the regime of the infamous communist dictator Nicholae Ceaucescu. He razed whole villages in the countryside and beautiful Parisian-style suburbs in Bucharest and replaced them with grey, concrete-block apartment towers. The Secret Police, who had spies everywhere, would arrest ordinary people without warning and torture them in the most degrading and terrible way.

Since the revolution of 1989, when Ceaucescu and his equally despicable wife, Elena Petrescu, were overthrown, Romania has striven towards a democratic government and is trying to rebuild itself. However, a lasting and moving legacy of Ceaucescu remains. He had hoped to double the population within ten years. Abortion was prohibited, as was contraception. If babies were born sickly or died, the doctors who delivered them were tortured. To maximise the babies' chances of survival, many considered at risk were given blood transfusions of unscreened blood. Ceaucescu would not admit that AIDS was present in Romania and so the blood was unscreened.

In a hospital in central Bucharest, children of eight, nine and ten years of age lie in cheerless wards in rusting iron cots. Many have been abandoned. They are rarely picked up or cuddled. Most have neither learnt to walk nor talk. They wave their hands compulsively in front of their faces – it is the only stimulation most of them get. They cower away from strangers. They have no toys or books. The staff are superstitiously afraid to give them even minimum attention. Their lives are measured in months rather than years and the outcome is in no doubt. Some are HIV positive, others have full-blown AIDS. They are the most innocent of victims. Momentarily, the world took an interest in their plight through television, but then forgot.

In a suburb of Bucharest, a Scottish nun and an English woman take me to a villa in a side street. There is a garden, a rabbit in a cage and inside children singing songs while an old man plays a piano accordion. In the kitchen the table is laid for lunch and in the bedrooms there are bunk beds each with a soft toy on them. The bathroom is impeccably clean and in every room the summer sun shines through the window. A shed at the end of the garden has been converted to a classroom.

These children are also HIV positive but they have been taken from the hospital and retrieved by the determined efforts of the English woman and the little band of nuns who are dedicated to seeing what love, good food, sunshine, play and intellectual stimulation can do for these children. Each child has a book with photographs and details, sometimes pitifully sparse, of his or her background and life. Some have succumbed to the ravages of the disease and are recorded in a special book. The Anglican vicar in Bucharest recently dedicated a memorial to those who died – a statue of an angel with outstretched wings and hands.

Every dollar that these two women can raise goes towards buying and refurbishing more houses. For those children still in the hospital, she tries to recruit volunteers to make sure they are never alone. However, the indifference of the Romanians to the suffering of others is monumental. Bucharest is full of beggars, starving cats and dogs, and thin donkeys pulling heavy carts. To a people who have endured so much, the lives of a group of doomed children are a matter for indifference.

However, in that house in the suburbs, the human spirit triumphed. I will never be able to forget those children or those women. Their dedication and their endurance, their humour and their hard work was humbling.

Lorraine Elliott

Give your love to others –
it might be all they have.

OUR GENTLE
TEACHER

The kitchen we sit in has lovely winter sunlight pouring through the large, north-facing window, but for Mum the light is not strong enough for her to see my face, my expression, or what I am wearing today. Her wonderful grey-blue eyes, which have seen so much change in the world, so much beauty, so much joy and so much adversity, can no longer see me, for she is now almost totally blind.

As a child she was always at home, always there for me, my seven sisters and three brothers, and of course our father. Our small suburban house was the centre of existence for Mum. It was her world, a place she and Dad had brought their family to to create a more prosperous life away from their war-ravaged homeland, the Netherlands.

As we discuss the upcoming celebrations for their sixtieth wedding anniversary, a strong sense of *déjà vu* settles over me as I remember with great clarity another anniversary party thirty-five years ago in this same house. I was only a small child but I recall thinking how old my parents were, when in fact they were still in their prime.

We loved our mother with an unreserved trust and unparalleled certainty that we would be loved in return. In my case this trust was well founded due to the enormous capacity my mother had, and continues to have, to love and care for all her children. Her love is limitless and selfless.

You would realistically envisage that once the bloom of new-found motherhood was spent, the feeling of elation when yet another baby arrived would quickly wane. But being towards the rear of the brood at number nine, I never felt her love was any less for me than for any other member of our family.

She could well have been a formidable diplomat, taking her place in the highest office of the land. She was able to negotiate, interrogate, subjugate and appease an endless barrage of family incidents continually staged by her children.

When you knew how kind and wonderful she was, you would really think twice about doing anything that might upset her, although we all still managed to get up to some terrible antics. I alone managed dramas ranging from conducting a real live bonfire (to roast chestnuts of course!) in the middle of the lounge-room floor at age ten, to escaping to meet friends in the middle of the night through my bedroom window at age fourteen.

She watched each of us grow to maturity and make our own future. She steered us all through childhood illnesses, adolescent rages and broken dreams. There were some very hard and often volatile times when the war of words engulfed and destabilised what was mostly a very close and supportive family unit.

We all learnt many things from the bad times as well as the good: communication, cooperation and resourcefulness, to name a few. Many responsibilities were shouldered by the older members of the family who contributed both financially and practically to the running of our home and the care of the younger children. This has possibly given us a stronger bond. A deeper connection and responsibility to each other has been forged through our mother's example of commitment.

The advancing years have seen my parents make enormous changes. Their roles have been reversed. My mother, the home-maker, the great organiser, the wonderful cook, the patient teacher, can no longer see. My father has learnt to care for her, to cook, to do the laundry, clean the house and attend to their weekly shopping, areas he certainly was very unfamiliar with having lived in a 'traditional' family structure all his life. My mother, who I never saw sit down unless she was shelling peas by the kitchen sink, is now unable to busy herself with her gardening, knitting or reading. It is a difficult time for them both.

When Mum spoke to me a short time ago about feeling useless and not having a purpose to her life any more, my reply was that every time I, or any of our now very extended family, sit with her and talk, reminisce or seek advice, she is there to offer an insight that I still find extraordinary.

She may no longer see our reactions, but she can sense our needs; that is a wonderful gift and one that in our high-tech, fast-paced life would be worth having with us forever – if only we could.

Yvonne Flynn (née Schreurs)

The measure of life is in what you give,
not in what you accumulate.

IN PRAISE OF
PALLIATIVE CARE

When the specialist finally gave a prognosis on my mother's life expectancy, we knew it would prove to be conservative. We had witnessed her at every monthly visit pleading with her once beautiful but now fading eyes: 'Doctor, please tell me.' But he had always gently declined to be specific. Finally, on 28 May 1993, he offered the opinion that she had less than two months to live.

When my father died two years earlier, my mother was already ill with cancer. Her illness was compounded with crippling arthritis, leading, over time, to two hip replacements. It wasn't long before living alone was impossible for her. My two sisters, two brothers and I were clear from her comments about my father's death that her preference would be to remain with the family. That ruled out putting her into institutionalised care, such as a nursing home. So my sister invited Mum to move in with her.

But it was not to be that simple. Mum was adamant that

she didn't want to put anyone out. A fiercely independent and highly intelligent woman, she had often expressed a deep fear of becoming a burden, and, even worse, of losing her mind.

What evolved as an inexhaustible commitment by my sister began with a slow and persistent process of persuading Mum that the offer for her to become an integral part of her home was real. Mum continued to waver as my sister had recently remarried and still had a teenage son living at home. Ultimately, as pain sapped her energy and incapacity loomed larger in her day-to-day battle for survival, Mum relented.

Inevitably there were difficulties in getting on together in the household: financial misunderstandings, demands of physical care and the practical problems arising out of the fact that my sister and her husband were both working. Thankfully ours wasn't the kind of family where there is conflict between the other sisters and brothers too.

Along the way my sister had started to call on the assistance of the Mid-Eastern Palliative Care Association (MEPCA). It started with the volunteers, who are carefully selected to assist with tasks such as shopping or banking, to help with hobbies or other leisure pursuits or to simply provide company.

Mum, among her many interests, had always been an insatiable Scrabble player. Now that films, theatre and concerts were beyond her strength, Scrabble became an even more important source of intellectual stimulation. 'The last thing I want is strangers fussing around me,' Mum said at first. But when MEPCA was able to provide an equally avid Scrabble-playing stranger, this became a tolerable intrusion and eventually an enjoyable and sustaining friendship. It set the pattern for the other MEPCA personnel who followed.

In time, qualified nursing support was also required and again MEPCA was there. Although Mum was typically sceptical at first, the nurses' visits became her lifeline and intrinsic to her sense of security. They had a network of communication with her local GP and, in turn, with her specialists. Anything untowards was immediately reported and acted upon. They came once a week and then twice, always making it clear they were on call at any time. Sometimes they arrived when Mum was asleep and, knowing she was deaf, they would return later to check on her and talk to her. They had no end of physical aids to make her more comfortable. They showered her and assisted her with various bodily functions. They monitored her medication like hawks. Their respect for her dignity was unlimited.

On a number of occasions when Mum was hospitalised, for chemotherapy amongst other things, they continued their caring through regular phone calls and inquiries.

And they supported my sister. If they visited when she wasn't there, they would ring her at work to see how she was managing. They rang regularly anyway just to keep in touch, but they were never intrusive. They stopped her from running herself into the ground.

We all agreed it was a wonderful service. But they had hardly got started.

With the specialist's prognosis confronting us, and Mum's condition distressing both her and us, questions arose as to whether she would be able to remain at home and whether there were ways in which we could ease her dying. The MEPCA nurses were realistic: 'No one knows what is going to happen. But we can tell you what to look for.'

Frequent visits became almost daily, sometimes just dropping in and other times extending to listening and providing advice on concerns. It was not always possible to have the same nurses, but those who came were always fully briefed in advance and equally compassionate. They saw a family strongly committed to a dying parent and, in their own understated way, they matched that commitment.

They advised us that it would not be long before Mum would be unable to cope with visitors. This enabled my sister to contact as many family members and friends as she could and, in what would have been Mum's own style, to shower them with hospitality when they arrived, as they duly did in droves. Unobtrusively, the MEPCA nurses would slip in and out, keeping a watchful eye.

In the final week, visits were confined to only the closest family members. By this time we were on 24-hour roster but we were confident that, with MEPCA's support, we would manage. Mum was unable to eat at all and freed of pain through morphine, and contact with her began to fade to the extent that we could not necessarily identify her needs. The MEPCA nurses were able to advise us on how to communicate and of the stages we could expect as she approached death. They dressed her wounds and administered medication to relieve her suffering. They instructed my sister on how to do so too.

Shortly after midnight on 23 June, Mum died with her family around her. One of the MEPCA nurses arrived within the hour. When the family was ready, the procedure of washing and laying out the corpse took place with my sister assisting. The fact that we knew the nurse quite well by then made this a consoling rather than a harrowing experience. And when Mum was restored again to a state of serenity, the nurse disappeared into the night.

Virginia Simmons

Giving love and dignity to others
enriches your life and theirs.

I MET AN
ANGEL

In 1968 I met an angel. I didn't know it at the time because, you see, I was asleep when she first visited me. Sometimes asleep, sometimes drugged, I was drifting in and out of consciousness for days. I'm told she was a constant visitor to the Royal Air Force hospital in the English Midlands where I was taken. An angel of mercy.

How was I to know? I didn't want to see anyone during those interminable weeks of operations. I spent the days assuring everyone around me that I was all right. I passed the never-ending nights holding hands with an Irish nurse whose soft, beautiful brogue comforted me as I cried out in self-recrimination, despair and disbelief. Why do we punish ourselves with self-blame?

Losing a husband in a fatal car accident and undergoing constant surgery had left me shattered and vulnerable. If only I hadn't agreed to travel overseas, if only I hadn't agreed to rent a car, if only I had insisted on driving when I could see him getting tired, if only . . .

There were no answers.

Realisation finally came that I was here whether I liked it or not, and then vanity set in. My face had to be reconstructed on one side and both jaws were broken. I was ashamed at how important it had become to have a face. The surgeons were wonderful and told me that many of the male patients were harder to handle. I explained that I didn't want to be Elizabeth Taylor, I just wanted to appear normal, so that four young children back home would know their mother.

One of the worst experiences during recovery was to find that when the metal and plaster were removed from my head, I had no hair! I had imagined that my long brown hair would fall down and hide the side of my face, which was covered in scars like tram lines.

'Never mind. The "Mia Farrow" look is in, Mrs Waite,' said one of the bright surgeons. Imagine the shock. The tiny stubble on my head with its newly formed grey patches was all too much. I cried. My sister, Bonnie, was wonderful. She had flown over from Australia to bring me home. She knew of a place in London where we could buy a wig.

This is when we met the angel.

Despite visiting the hospital, washing my clothes, liaising with the hospital's CEO and eventually lending me that important wig, we had never met. It appears that when the news of our accident reached Australia, an acquaintance of mine from the children's school contacted her friend in Shropshire, Claude Reed, who turned out to be my angel.

An attractive, vivacious woman, Claude had been an eighteen-year-old French girl when she married John Reed, the Sheriff of Shropshire. A devout Catholic, she could hardly speak

English but quickly learnt to cope with home management on a large estate, caring for tenants and two small daughters. She was, and is, warm, generous, kind and strong. She took my sister and me into her heart and her home. I was fragile and somewhat battered in mind and body. Claude and her lovely daughter, Caroline, nursed and nourished me until the time came to travel home by ship.

We laughed together, we cried together and Claude's wonderful husband, John, helped me with details of the inquest and arrangements I couldn't face. He wouldn't hear of my sister and me staying anywhere else and was fascinated with our tales of Australia and the outback.

Despite my condition, my memories of this time remain vivid. Can you imagine being taken to an ivy-covered mansion where the dog slept in front of the fire, a nightingale sang in a tree above the croquet lawn and you slept in a four-poster bed with every conceivable comfort nearby? I remember the little books and the fine antique china on my tray which had to be brought upstairs every day with the best silver and tiny biscuits. I can remember a glass of sherry being miraculously produced whenever I looked wan. I remember so many, many things. Despite my grief, it was a fairytale scene that will remain indelible in my memory.

Years later, on another visit, I said to Claude, 'You didn't even know me. How could you have done this for just anyone?'

Her reply was swift, 'I didn't do it for just anyone!'

Noel Waite

Everyone is deserving of unconditional love.

EVERY
CONVERSATION
COUNTS

I remember the phone call well. I was in the car, hurrying. No, not hurrying, rushing from my home to one of several business appointments. It was late on a Tuesday afternoon and I was simply 'flat to the boards'. I was under incredible stress; my second child, Victoria, had just been born, I'd been away from the office, I was way overworked and I felt stressed. On top of the work pressures and the new baby I had marital problems as well. I look back now and wonder: 'How did I make it? Was it all worth it?' It was just so stressful, but at the time I just accepted it.

The car phone rang and it was my father. He was ringing to discuss a simple issue — about coming over to visit the baby — but before I knew it, I'd let loose. I told him everything that was bothering me, and on top of it all I said to him, 'Dad, I'm simply bored with it all.' Well, in the few moments he got a word in (somewhere in between my complaints and negativity), I could hear my dad's enthusiasm slowly dwindling. By the end of the conversation he had forgotten about the purpose of his call, to visit his grandchild. At a time when I'm sure he hoped I would be elated with my child, I was moaning and complaining and must have seemed very unhappy.

When the conversation was over I felt better – well, a tiny bit better – at having voiced some of my problems. But my dad seemed to be feeling worse. I'd transferred my stress on to his shoulders, which was the last thing a man retiring after a long career needed. He wanted to relax, to enjoy his grandchildren, and his favourite leisure activity – sailing.

The next day I was still feeling rather stressed, so I made some time to go shopping. It really didn't matter what I was buying, I just wanted to get away from everything for a couple of hours and be in a bright, positive environment. I remember my spirits were raised, just a little bit.

While I was shopping I knew Dad was off sailing. He was sailing across Port Phillip Bay to place his boat in a dry dock at Phillip Island. I knew Mum was driving down to the island to meet him with coffee and sandwiches and to take him home. I arrived home at about eleven o'clock that morning and within minutes my sister was on the phone with the shocking news that my father had died after suffering a massive coronary at Phillip Island.

I broke down, crying and sobbing and wishing, as so many people do, that I'd had the chance to say goodbye. My heart was wrenched out because not only did I miss the opportunity to say goodbye, but my last conversation with my father was so negative.

I used to take it for granted that I would see someone the next day or the day after or the day after that. Now I realise that you never know if you'll see a friend, a family member or an acquaintance ever again. I realise the importance of uplifting others in my conversations and not dragging them down with my problems. It's best to leave my problems, I've learnt, for counselling.

Knowing this does not take away the twinges of guilt and sadness I still feel today after leaving my poor father with all my problems.

Sue Calwell

Always be loving and uplifting
and you will live
without regrets.

TAKING ACTION

GIVING OF YOURSELF

❧

Use this Action Planner to turn the messages in this

chapter into reality in your life. Turn to pages xvi–xvii to

learn the six simple steps you need to know to make the

most of this Action Planner and to enhance your life.

ACTION STEP

Become a volunteer, coach a children's sporting team,
help at a hospital or aged person's home, assist at your library.
Donating your time is far more valuable and rewarding than
donating your money.

MY SPECIFIC ACTION STEP

....
....
....
....
....

ACTION STEP

Find a person with a genuine need and replace the shallow words
'If you need help just call me' with action. Be perceptive, have
empathy, discover what the person requires and do it – tune their
car, cut their grass, babysit their children . . . just arrive on their
doorstep prepared to help.

MY SPECIFIC ACTION STEP

....
....
....
....
....

ACTION STEP

Write a letter to a child explaining all the things
you love about them. Give the letter to the child as
a special gift.

MY SPECIFIC ACTION STEP

....

....

....

....

....

....

ACTION STEP

Reach out to a lonely person in your community.
Do this formally through a program such as 'Big Brother'
or do it yourself. There are so many people out there
who need to be loved.

MY SPECIFIC ACTION STEP

....

....

....

....

....

ACTION STEP

Instead of selling raffle tickets, buy the whole book
and give the tickets away.

MY SPECIFIC ACTION STEP

....

....

....

....

....

....

....

ACTION STEP

Organise a neighbourhood working bee for an
elderly person in your area.

MY SPECIFIC ACTION STEP

....

....

....

....

....

....

....

ACTION STEP

Telephone someone who means a great deal to you but who you haven't contacted for a while. Work at your friendships – they require giving as well as taking – and the rewards will be invaluable.

MY SPECIFIC ACTION STEP

....
....
....
....
....
....

ACTION STEP

Give a bunch of flowers or a small gift to a friend,
not because it's their birthday or because they're feeling down,
just because you value them.

MY SPECIFIC ACTION STEP

....
....
....
....
....
....

CHANGING PRIORITIES

*Go placidly amid the noise and haste
and remember what peace
there may be in silence.*

STRIKING A BALANCE

One of the most difficult feats for an executive or business person is the juggling of quality time between career and family. My career path was clearly defined and very focused from the outset. While I have certainly enjoyed and played my sport to a very competitive level, career development and success were always number one.

Marriage to Isabell in 1971 saw both of us following careers for the first few years before we endeavoured to have a family. After six years of tests and futile attempts at artificial insemination, we put our names down for adoption. In 1979 our son Rhys arrived and our lives changed dramatically and had new meaning.

At that time I was general manager for a multinational recruitment consultancy in New Zealand and, in 1982, we achieved another of our dreams – a small hobby farm. Two days after moving on to the property we were asked to transfer to Melbourne. Prior to accepting we made special arrangements with the local social welfare agency to keep our place on the priority waiting list for a second child. We transferred to Melbourne just in time to hit the 1982–83 recession! Our dream farmlet took six months to sell and we subsequently lived in four locations before securing our own home. Worse still, on arrival we found the company virtually insolvent and losing big dollars.

The next nine months involved travelling throughout Australia, rationalising the total operation and working through more damage-control procedures. Times were difficult due to the company's financial problems and to our not having sold our own property. Relief finally arrived with the sale of our New Zealand property five months later. We had turned the corner – the company was beginning to trade profitably, we had our own home, and we were establishing a lifestyle. Then one day we received a call to say that we had been removed from the priority list due to the chronic shortage of children available for adoption and because we no longer resided in New Zealand. We looked at the options: we were too old to adopt in Australia (the waiting list was five to seven years) and could not adopt from Indonesia both because Australia had experienced some major immigration problems from earlier Indonesian adoptions and because we were living in Australia on New Zealand passports. It was decision time. What should we do?

We decided that I should resign my position and return to New Zealand and take our chances on the priority list for adoption – there were no guarantees. Many of my business colleagues and friends could not believe I could abandon what appeared to be an enviable career. We sold our home (at a loss), purchased an old two-bedroom wooden house in Christchurch, borrowed money from the bank and established a new recruitment firm. It was six months from the date of our last pay cheque before the business received its first 'cash in'. We had lost half of our capital having sold in depressed markets in both Australia and New Zealand.

During our first six to eight months in business, I budgeted $10 a week for my own personal expenses (I don't know how Isabell managed) and was actually seen travelling to and from the office on public transport (a far cry from the executive vehicle and other benefits in my previous role). Times were tough, but very exciting, and the company quickly became successful – fear of failure is a great motivator.

In October 1984, great joy! Our daughter Kim came along to complete our family – the gamble had paid off!

We now live on our new dream property and are enjoying the fruits of our labour and, most of all, our family. We learnt that it's what you *do* that's important in life, not what you *have*. Another lesson learnt through these times was that at some point in your life, you have to come to terms with yourself and determine what it is you really want – what is precious to you and how you want to live. We made our choices together, our lives are much richer for having done so, and we are better people as a result.

Barry Knight

When making major choices, be guided by what is most precious to you.

THE HEART
RULES

I first met Eve, a six-year-old with exquisite features and a beautiful nature, in March 1992. The main thing that struck me was how quiet and withdrawn she was. Not that I should have been surprised – she had lost her mother to cancer less than a year before.

At the age of five, Eve and her three-year-old brother Jarvis had been left stranded. I couldn't even begin to comprehend how they must have felt to lose the affection, the touch and the gentle voice of their mum, the caring person who was supposed to 'always be there' for them. Those feelings don't just disappear, especially for such young children for whom death must be so confusing.

The months went by and in March 1993 their father Daniel and I became engaged to be married. During this time I got to know Eve more, but the more I talked to her, observed her and cuddled her the sadder she seemed to get. She never talked about her mum and never cried about missing her; even on the wedding day she put on a brave face. She kept all her anger and her sadness inside.

After Daniel and I married, I really felt an obligation as the 'new mum' to help Eve and Jarvis with their grieving, so I suggested we get a puppy. I had no experience with death or with children, but I knew that a puppy would provide them with unconditional love and companionship. A puppy would be a special friend they could hug and cuddle through their times of confusion and sadness.

So we searched and found Fenwick, a six-week-old English setter. He slept on the beds, we took him on walks, we took him in the car everywhere we went and the kids dressed him up. He was a much needed part of the family (there's no such thing as a 'step dog'!) and he brought lots of smiles to Eve and Jarvis.

After a year passed, Eve adopted a new pet, a baby ringtail possum found in our garden. She became mum to the possum, keeping it snug in her jumper, feeding it and letting it sleep in her room. It really brought out Eve's caring, gentle nature. However, possums are nocturnal and for our sanity we had to take Eve's tiny possum to a wildlife care network. We did this without consultation with Eve.

That day when Eve got home from school Daniel and I saw something in Eve that we'd never seen before. Eve was distraught, and crying uncontrollably. It seemed that finally, three years after her mother's death, she was letting out some of the hurt.

A few months later we brought another dog into our lives, a golden cocker spaniel named Honey, who we brought home from the pound.

About nine months later we decided to sell up everything and move to America. So apart from selling the house, all our furniture and the cars, there was the practicality of taking the dogs (or, as most people warned us, the *impracticality* of taking a whole family and two dogs to another country when we didn't even have a roof over our heads!). So our trusty, faithful, fun-loving dogs had to be given away.

I kept trying to rationalise our decision, to justify it to myself even though I was torn between doing the practical thing and wanting to keep the dogs. Daniel and I boldly went on with our daily activities. I noticed Eve became quieter and quieter, sadder and sadder. Honey found a new home quickly, which took us by surprise. The day after Honey left I watched, feeling helpless, as Eve curled up next to Fenwick on his smelly dog's bed and let out the most heart-wrenching cries of sadness, loneliness and helplessness I had ever heard. This was more than tears for a lost dog – Eve was crying for Honey, for her mum, for her possum and everything else she had lost that was dear to her. And there was Fenwick to comfort her.

Moving Fenwick to America became a decision that, no matter how costly, couldn't be based only on making our lives easier. Once more, the emotional benefits of keeping Fenwick, especially for Eve, far outweighed the practical ones that would make Daniel's and my life easier. Needless to say, Fenwick came to America with us.

During this time I realised Eve and Jarvis needed more than the love and affection a dog could give them. Daniel and I applied for me to adopt the children and become their 'new' mum. It was a very extensive, drawn-out process but it was probably the proudest day of my life when, on 28 June 1996, Daniel and I stood in court with Eve and Jarvis and I became their mother forever. Fenwick, of course, was waiting in the car.

Kate Johnson

Switching focus from your own needs
to the needs of others
brings out the best in you.

An Unexpected Career Change

My story covers an unexpected career change, and one which proved to be the most devastating experience of my life.

I commenced a banking career in 1960 and, following twenty-nine years of successful service with one of Australia's leading banks, I was head-hunted for the job of executive director to a leading regional bank. While many challenging and exciting developments took place in those early days, they all paled into insignificance when compared with the ill-fated fraudulent sale of two insurance companies.

The impact of this bizarre event on my life was dramatic, to say the least. As the acting chief executive officer at the time (the CEO was overseas), I oversaw and signed off on a series of transactions involving the proposed sale of two life insurance companies from their then owner to what was shortly thereafter revealed to be a fraudulent buyer. Clearly there were underlying factors that never emerged, or were never allowed to surface in the subsequent court hearings. The fact that the transactions were not reversed immediately following the detection that there was no 'real' buyer, remains a mystery. What in fact happened was a costly Supreme Court case extending over six months and costing the various parties in excess of $25 million.

This brief story can never even attempt to portray the complicity of those events, suffice to say though, justice was not seen to be served, a belief shared by many who were closer to the inner sanctums of this debacle than me.

During the period of the court case, for which I was the principal witness, I experienced the most daunting period in my life. Facing the most experienced and highly credentialled QCs in the business (in all there were about seventeen QCs), I was subjected to the most demeaning and torturous cross-examination. This relentless and seemingly endless saga extended over a week without any let-up whatsoever. Every night I would journey home feeling mentally exhausted and spiritually crushed. My self-esteem was almost irreparably damaged by this vigilant pursuit on the part of the defending parties to twist and contort the focus away from the principal issue, which was the fraudulent sale of these two insurance companies.

It would be imprudent for me to discuss the underlying reasons or the real beneficiaries of this bizarre event. Let's just say that in this instance justice was not served, and that reputations were severely damaged, but not necessarily those most deserving of damage.

During this whole episode my mother was dying of cancer. I have no doubt this saga brought that fateful event to an earlier-than-expected conclusion. We were extremely close and my mother felt all this additional pain and emotional suffering with me.

After my resignation from the bank I made some rather poorly judged investment decisions – a tendency, I have since come to learn, which invariably accompanies emotional traumas of this magnitude. Fortunately, I drew on all my inner strength and, with the support of friends (the ones who remain with you through these ill-fated periods in your life), I set about rebuilding my personal esteem and pursuit of a life that would embrace real values.

Ironically, fate had its way in drawing me to a profession that was dedicated to helping and supporting employees who have lost their jobs. My personal experience, coupled with the extensive training that my employer has provided in outplacement, has enabled me to assist other managers and executives in their transition to new employment, and provided me with a challenging new career that is also personally gratifying.

I met a wonderful lady who is now my wife, and life has taken on a whole new chapter – one that is built around values and relationships that are meaningful and important.

Our careers can often change without our choosing, but with the right attitude, this can often be for the better.

Bryan Waters

*View every life change as an opportunity
to make your life more fulfilling.*

HURRY
SICKNESS

In 1992, John Murphy died after suffering the ravages of cancer for several years. John had been a mentor for most of my adult life and I valued his advice and guidance as well as his friendship over some forty years.

Sometime in 1989, when John first became aware of his limited time, we had a long discussion about our lives, which had been similar. We had joined the army from school, spent some thirty years as officers both in and out of Australia, including some operational service in Malaya and Vietnam, and then we both spent some time in the Victorian Public Service and were members of Legacy. Our discussion covered such things as where we had been, what we had done, what we had achieved and how, in part, we might have done it better.

Over the previous several months John said he had been very reflective about his life. During our lengthy discussion he voiced what had been some of his most contemplative thoughts. While his own life wasn't perfect, he had drawn some conclusions and come up with some constructive ideas which he thought others might also find useful. What he said had a profound effect on me and how I have subsequently viewed my own life. He certainly gave me a lot to think about and, in turn, I would like to share some of John's thoughts and words with you.

He felt our world seemed to be going crazy. It had become like a giant treadmill that was moving so fast people were finding it difficult to get off. It seemed to him that in every human endeavour, there was a demand for things to be done faster, and that, to satisfy ever-expanding expectations, people were forced to use an increasingly complex range of technical assistance. He labelled this phenomenon 'hurry sickness' and attributed many of today's health and social problems to this sickness: stress-related disorders, broken marriages and friendships, broken homes and homeless children. He believed that much of the intolerance, impatience and selfishness that we see around us could also be traced to hurry sickness.

John seemed quite clear about what was causing this sickness and the toll it was having on our society. He saw our personal desire for continual acquisition, particularly of money and material things, as being at least partly responsible and that this, in turn, was leading us into unhealthy lives and increasing our chances of an early death. Hurry sickness was de-humanising us and making us insensitive to much of what happens around us. He saw that many people didn't appear to have the time to stop and take stock of their lives. If they did, he argued, they might be able to see their deteriorating personal situation and how their collective neglect was causing our society a great deal of hurt.

After much discussion, John and I decided it was important to take stock regularly – at least once a year. We deduced a list of goals for a healthy life. If we at least try to achieve these goals, we will be combating hurry sickness. I have called this 'John's List', and it follows:

JOHN'S LIST

- Maintain a set of personal values and standards.
- Demonstrate self-discipline and self-control.
- Be responsible and accountable for your actions.
- Look after your health and maintain a good level of physical and mental fitness.
- Manage your stress in a realistic and practical way.
- Have balance and quality in your life – don't perpetually battle the clock.
- Be considerate, unselfish and tolerant of others.
- Be co-operative and helpful to others.
- Work at maintaining the family unit.
- Cultivate a circle of friends who are trustworthy and dependable.
- Make a personal contribution to the community in which you live.

As a tribute to John's memory, I am hoping that readers of this piece might use John's List as a guide for taking stock of their own lives and perhaps doing something constructive about their own hurry sickness.

Ian Teague

Money can't buy you health, love and quality of life.

Man in the Mirror

Sometimes it takes a 40-ton truck to hit you square on before you realise that you may be headed in the wrong direction. I was forty when mine hit.

After helping to build a thirty-five-office real-estate network in Melbourne in the midst of a recession, I found myself working seven days a week and not really enjoying it. Married with four children already in their teens, I came home one night at the normal time (about eight-thirty) and told my second eldest, a boy of thirteen, to go and do something (I can't remember what it was). He turned to me and told me to go and get —— and then proceeded to give it to me with both barrels.

My initial reaction was of course to throttle him and justify why I was never at his school or following his sport, et cetera, et cetera, and how I was doing it all for them. Fortunately, cooler heads prevailed and instead of thumping him I sent him to his room. Later that night I sat with my wife Jenny and we started discussing some of those big questions in life: Where are we going? Why? What's the purpose of it all? Who and what do we love in life? The next day when I arrived at work I found this poem on my desk:

When you get what you want in your struggle for self,
And the world makes you king for a day,
Just go to a mirror and look at yourself,
And see what that man has to say.
For it isn't your father, or mother or wife,
Whose judgement upon you must pass,
The fellow whose verdict counts most in your life,
Is the one looking back in the glass.
Some people may call you a straight-shooting chum,
And call you a wonderful guy,
But the man in the glass says you're only a bum,
If you can't look him straight in the eye.
He's the fellow to please — never mind all the rest —
For he's with you clear up to the end.
And you've passed your most dangerous, difficult test,
If the man in the glass is your friend.
You may fool the whole world down the pathway of life,
And get pats on the back as you pass,
But your final reward will be heartache and tears
If you've cheated the man in the glass!

Three weeks later I was out of the business. I chose to follow my passion to help others 'perform at their highest level'. It took three years to redevelop my relationship with my son and the rest of the family. I thank God for that truck!

John Lockwood

Take the time to assess your priorities.

DISCOVERING
'ME'

For my entire adult years I've been an extremely dedicated chief executive, with staff reporting to me and personal assistants to handle all the 'details' of my life. During my late thirties and the most demanding segment of my career, I had three wonderful children. In 1995 I decided to finish full-time employment and broaden my life by concentrating on being a full-time mother. I wasn't prepared for the shock!

Just figuring out how I fit into the school community has been a great challenge. It might seem an easy thing to do, to talk to other parents, drop off and pick up your children from school and organise social events — and should have been easy for a former CEO used to dealing with people of every persuasion — but I found it very difficult.

As soon as I left my position, I started receiving comments from people like: 'Didn't you used to be Sue Calwell?' (to which I'd respond, 'Well, actually I still *am* Sue Calwell!') or 'We hear you're not working now. What do you do?' They would walk away or obviously switch off when they heard I was a full-time mother. After I'd heard comments like these a few times, it began to sink in that I needed to rediscover just who Sue Calwell really was.

I began the journey by first discovering my own 'estranged' children. I use the term 'estranged' because they'd been brought up in the main by nannies, grandparents, friends and helpers. While I'd always been there for their special times, my job took me away from Melbourne regularly, and the domestic issues of school lunches, school clothes (matching socks!) homework and after-school curricula were way beyond the number of hours in my day.

During that time I'd thought of Sue Calwell as a CEO – her personality and life was reflected in that role. However, through my children's love I have discovered that I am Sue Calwell, a person, who was fortunate enough to spend twenty years in a ful-filling and demanding career role and is still fortunate enough to have a loving and supporting family. I am so thankful that I can now see and appreciate the difference between the two Sues.

When I left behind my CEO role I noticed the invitations to functions suddenly drop away like rocks falling off the edge of a cliff. I was no longer asked to attend openings and key Melbourne events. I realise now that the organisers weren't inviting Sue Cal-well, they were inviting the position. This understanding has made it easier to let go of the trappings that went with that position.

The scary thing is that back in the old days I'm sure that my children thought I was too busy to bother with their problems, and sometimes I wasn't even in town when they needed some spe-cial nurturing. Thank goodness I'm now able to spend time with them. They have so much to offer! Through them I have learnt that

I am lovable not for what I do, or for what I was perceived to be, but for who I am. They have taught me the value of unconditional love and that every person, in every way, is important.

Sue Calwell

Love yourself, not for what you do or
have done but for who you are.

A FACE IN THE CROWD

The murmur of the capacity audience had just faded into expectant silence. This was one of the most important days in little five-year-old Patricia McKee's life: the Kernot School Concert. Her heart raced as she stood behind the curtain. Yet she was not afraid because everyone had been rehearsing for weeks and knew their parts by heart. The lead-up over the last few days had almost been unbearable.

Being in an isolated country town, Patricia knew that everyone would turn out for the big occasion – everyone! Yet, it was this awareness that tinged her excitement with sadness. There were two people who wouldn't be in that audience, couldn't be in that audience, that night – her mum and dad.

Patricia's mother and father ran the local general store, which doubled as the post office and manual telephone exchange. It was a 24-hour commitment – an urgent call could come through at any time of the day or night. It was simply accepted that Mum and Dad could never attend community activities since someone had to mind the store. It had been this way with her sister, so why should it be any different for her? Still, she couldn't help wishing that her mum and dad could be there to see her on such a special day, so she'd decided to broach the subject with her mother.

Only now, as a parent herself, does Patricia really understand the deep pain in her mother's response: 'I'll try and be there, sweetheart, but you know how hard it is for us to get away from the store.' Even at such a tender age, Patricia did know how difficult it was and resigned herself to the fact that her parents wouldn't be there.

Yet as the curtain slowly opened on the stage of the Kernot Hall all those years ago, little Patricia McKee got the surprise of her life. There, sitting four rows from the front, was her mother 'with a smile on her face from ear to ear'!

This vivid image remains one of Patricia's most cherished memories. 'Words cannot express the sheer joy we both experienced at that moment. I was so happy I was walking on air. All my prayers had been answered.'

Patricia's parents have since passed away, but what a wonderful legacy they've left us: when your children really need you, be there for them and you'll both be the richer for it.

Laurie Smale

When a loved one really needs you,
be there for them.

SUPER·MUM

Somewhere in the insanity of the eighties, the term 'superwoman' surfaced and I was determined to join the ranks. After all, I had the qualifications: three children under three, a husband, a business, plus a couple of almost house-trained pets. Most importantly, I knew it would be a piece of cake and that I'd be first on the podium to accept my trophy for 'Superwoman of the Year'. The worried looks and 'Don't do its!' from family and friends only served to spirit me on. I was ready to take on the challenge.

In the early days I learnt quickly – give the kids something to do during the 10-kilometre trek from creche to home. They were tired and cranky and needed distracting. Simple answer – food. This worked well for the first five minutes, but boredom quickly set in. Sandwiches began to fly from one end of the car to the other. At the end of the first week the car looked like tip, and smelt even worse. I never wanted to see another sandwich again!

Still the lessons continued . . . I'd been looking forward to attending a major fashion event. People like Ita Buttrose, Sally Browne and Adele Palmer would be there – all my career role models. That morning I dressed in my favourite black suit so I could go to the event straight from work. By five o'clock I was in a mad hurry, feeding baby Adrian with one hand and taking notes with the other while balancing the phone on my shoulder. At the same time a salesman was showing me a new range of fabrics. He commented on how quickly the baby was eating. One more gulp and Adrian had swallowed the last mouthful. I quickly handed him to my husband, but not quickly enough – I was now soaked to my underwear in baby vomit. The salesman made a quick exit. I scrounged through the factory to find something else to wear and managed to throw an outfit together – but I had no underwear. I went to the presentation and sat with my arms folded and legs crossed for the entire evening.

I remember saying to a friend, 'Hey, three kids and a business, it's not going to change my life.' I was so wrong! It took a bevy of well-timed lessons (most often involving my kids) to realise that the term 'superwoman' obviously originated in some late-night American sitcom. There was no such being in the real world. Success in life (for men and women) means having the courage to ask for help, sharing the load and working as a team. I learnt that to be a good mum, a thoughtful wife and a successful businesswoman was truly achievable when I no longer saw the need to do it all on my own.

Faye Browne

*Don't be afraid to ask for help – it can
bring balance into your life.*

LIFE IS A DECISION

My early childhood is a jumble of memories: making peg dolls with painted faces, all clothed in crepe paper; my feet pedalling my grandmother's treadle sewing machine; painting vivid blue skies over gold fields, gum trees and fence posts, all in perspective; using white shoe cleaner to make my paints go further; using baby powder make-up on my friends for plays on our back verandah.

Later I recall spending hours designing a round house; entering and being accepted for the then prestigious *Herald* Outdoor Art Exhibition with a painting of an art show; being denied the use of mother's new Singer sewing machine until I am twelve; staying awake all night designing my summer wardrobe (my first collection?), which I imagined making with an allowance of £4 a week (not allowed); cutting my first pattern from newspaper (a copy of a top later returned to the local shop).

We stuff our bras, wasp our waists, girdle our bottoms,

beehive our hair, high-heel our feet, pancake our faces and empty our heads in efforts to transform/conform/deform ourselves into images of Monroe, Loren and Mansfield. Declaring that I will never marry young, I turn away, imagining the women of Blooms-bury and freedom of association, while schoolfriends haunt jewellers' windows admiring engagement rings.

The school curriculum demands I choose between my favourite subjects: maths and art, thus precluding architecture. Fear of 'girls' jobs' (nursing, teaching and typing) moves me away from psychology, and my parents' mental image of artists starving in garrets precludes my ambition to become a painter. At fifteen I stumble into the School of Art at the Royal Melbourne Institute of Technology (not interior design) and choose printed textiles (not painting) as my major. Fellow student Leslie Dumbrell, now a lead-ing abstract artist, heads a delegation, saying, 'You should change your course to painting.'

While privately studying draping (as opposed to paper pattern-making) and working on Friday afternoons at a small dress-makers/factory, I sew for friends and family and make myself a new dress each week (my mother sewing up the hem while boys wait to take me out). Young friends predict I will become the Mary Quant of Australia.

However, nothing prepares me for the success that comes my way nor warns me I will give up youth's freedom. I achieve fame, fortune, friends and family; fabulous? Absolutely! I work incredibly long hours, I travel the world, jet-setting, high with the fun of creating, the joy of being part of great international teams of marketeers, manufacturers, administrators, designers and artists. And yet?

In my mid-thirties, a midlife crisis: at the end of a summer's day spent body-surfing, jogging and meeting new minds, I realise I have no means to answer the simple question, 'What do I want?' Then follows what has become a life quest, starting with the study of gestalt therapy (the German word *gestalt* means 'the whole picture'), yoga and meditation. On my thirty-ninth birthday I suddenly understand what 'life begins at forty' means. I realise that my life begins when I accept no one but myself is responsible for what happens to me.

The ambition to paint burns deep inside me. I return to life drawing, at night at Swinburne college, regaining my hand after years of directing a team of artists and designers. At a business party in Melbourne, Clif (he hated Pugh) arrives in a black mini coat, sans thongs. Excited, he is just back from the Kimberleys with a new combination of colour: 'red-gold' and 'blue-green-grey'. He asks me to come and look: 'Come for breakfast tomorrow at 8 a.m.' On this sunny hot humid December morning a business associate and I drive up to Dunmoochin via Hurstbridge. We swim; breakfast is coffee only. Clif shows his field studies; the colours sing. Back to the city, breakfasting on the way. The next Saturday I find I cannot *not* go back to Dunmoochin. I feel drugged. I am compelled to return. Clif and I arrange a painting trip after Christmas, with friends on the east coast. This is the first of many painting trips we take together.

Business in the eighties is increasingly tough, demanding my full attention. Finally, after six years of procrastination, I decide to close the fashion business. I want to travel in the outback, to paint more. Just before I announce my decision and two years after I had started painting, Clif dies. I leave work late with the sun's long red rays, and I understand; dying teaches us living.

For some time I hear Clif's voice as I continue to paint in his last studio at Dunmoochin. His voice gradually fades. A self-portrait shows me golden yet sad. Clif always painted himself when he wanted to clarify his direction. I continue this today. I cannot go back. I close my business. Neither of my daughters at that time wants to take it on. Almost thirty years is well and good.

Returning to art school is not feasible. I ask new artist friends, 'Who is the best painting teacher?' I always seek the best guide. That day a name comes up many times, Merv Moriarty. John Traynor comes to lunch and explains that Clif's next outback tour to Palm Valley will now be led by Merv. I recall many stories of a flying artist/teacher Clif had toured with through the Queensland outback and the islands on behalf of Gough Whitlam's fledgling Australia Council.

I have found my painting-teacher/mentor/fellow-artist/life-partner. Now Merv Moriarty and I live high on the Monaro in south-eastern New South Wales painting. I am not missing fashion.

Can I ever say I regret the career that led me into so many people's lives? I have no regrets. But is this true? What if I had stayed and lived in New York? Or what if I had spent more time with my daughters, Tiffany and Atlanta? Perhaps if I had studied painting from the age of fifteen I would now be a recognised master . . . Who knows, and who cares; life is the decision I make, now.

Prue Acton

Life begins when you accept that you
are responsible for your own destiny –
take charge now.

HEADY TIMES

I'm a musician/composer, and a fairly good one, having enjoyed success at a level that gave me an income I'd never dreamed of, but at some point during my success I forgot what I was.

They say it's time to get out of the share market when your taxi driver starts advising you on investment. Well, I was advising the taxi driver, so to speak.

I thought I was a property developer, a timber-mill operator, a cruise boat operator, a hotel owner, a restaurateur, et cetera. In fact, everything but what I was actually good at – writing music. My time was taken up overseeing a little out-of-control empire, sitting in boardrooms and conferences discussing things I mostly didn't understand.

But, I felt important: I drove a flash car, had a flash boat and felt I had risen above my housing commission origins and the stigma of being 'just a muso'. I had respect, or so I thought.

Suddenly all that changed. My 'respectable' empire started to implode and it wasn't long before I was standing before my creditors begging forgiveness. I avoided bankruptcy but I had nothing: no houses, no cars, no income, no confidence, no future.

Then, something good happened. I remembered who I was. I remembered that I could write songs and play an instrument, so I went back to my roots and formed a band. The band became moderately successful and my confidence started to creep back – I discovered I could still 'cut the mustard'.

I started to enjoy the little things, like finding a bargain, discovering public transport, seeking out cheap eating places. Enjoying open and public places without feeling the need to buy them. Life became simpler and even as I got busier with my work I experienced a calm that has stayed with me.

These days I'm as busy as ever but my life is not cluttered by unnecessary and unwanted self-aggrandisement. I am only interested in things to which my skills are relevant, and when, on occasions, someone comes to me with a deal or a proposition, I always ask four questions of myself: Is it to do with music? Do I know anything about it? Do I need it? Will it improve my life? The answer is usually no.

Mike Brady

Simplify your life – it will reduce stress and
give you more time to be joyful.

FLYING ART

Twenty-five years younger than I am now, I took off on a solo flight around Queensland, with my one-week-old pilot's licence and my mission to provide an art school to country Queensland and northern New South Wales. I don't really know why I started the flying art school, especially since, some years earlier, I had asked to be rescued from a commitment to teaching art so that I might concentrate on my own painting. At the time, my asking was answered in the usual roundabout way that life seems to favour and, after some absurd blind alleys, I began a three-year contract to paint for Rudy Komon.

Three years and two exhibitions later, the contract with Rudy was over and I was between the end of something and the beginning of some other yet-to-be-defined thing. My life to this point had defined me as an artist and art teacher and I knew that my next move would include teaching, but for some inexplicable reason, all the usual avenues were unacceptable to me.

With my partner in life then, later to be my second wife, Helen Brownsden, I indulged in that most potent of all of life's lotteries, the brainstorm. On my piece of paper I had written (along with a list of less ridiculous ideas) a flying art school. I thought then that this foolish idea had fallen aimlessly out of the sky and onto my paper, but on reflection I realised it was prompted unknowingly by country students at uni summer schools, a flight in a Cessna 180 and also by the absurd idea, embedded deep in my subconscious, that I could bring an understanding of art to people, previously denied this language by the inadequacies of a preoccupied and distracted society.

The first wings of the flying art school were not made of metal and driven by an engine-powered propeller, they grew out of the need to speak – to speak of things beyond the reach of words, of things to do with the spirits sinking and rising with the sun, of the colours in the clouds and of the joys and the heartbreaks of life.

This need to speak seemed to be felt more by women than men, who lived in a world where physical needs were an everyday reality and psychological needs an illusion. They needed someone to start something to which they could belong, empowered with a new language and a canvas, and I was picked on to do my best, whatever others might judge that to be. I became a slave to this 'something', this art school, not resentfully but willingly, utterly enamoured of it and all that it promised. The school became the purpose and the battleground for the next twelve years of my life as we struggled from success to crisis and from crisis to success. Sadly (or is it joyfully?) most of the crises were about money, power and the ability to continue; and most of the successes were more private and personal.

People awoke to a greater and broader world where art

rejected its definition as trivial wall decoration and became the shape and colour of life, more wonderful and more frightening than it had ever been before – it has, after all, the power to make its maker. All sorts of people discovered that they were responsible for the marks they made, and I learnt as they learnt. Then other people joined in to lend a shoulder to the wheel and it grew in strength. Then suddenly it was all official, with a board, and for Helen and myself it was less painful and we grew flowers and raised chickens between trips. Then it changed again, and again, and then it was all gone, and I was off to Melbourne to start life all over again.

Now, when I talk to the people around my chosen part of the world, I am filled with doubt. Through their eyes I see no need for art – life goes on perfectly well without it. Yet when I stand in an art gallery or at a concert, grabbed by the chest and thrust up by some great work of art, someone (perhaps outwardly smiled upon by life's fortunes) will drift past, unmoved, and I know I have no doubt.

Mervyn Moriarty

Life is empty without a passion.

THE ULTIMATE SACRIFICE

Linda Birdish was an outstanding American teacher who decided that when she had the time she would write lots of poetry and paint many pictures. Tragically, when she was twenty-eight she began to suffer severe headaches and her doctors discovered she had developed a massive brain tumour. They told her that her chance of surviving an operation was only 2 per cent and that if they didn't operate, she would have only six months to live.

Linda knew she had to express the artistic talents she had welling inside her, so for the next six months she wrote and painted furiously to bring out the beautiful gifts she held within. All that she wrote was published except for one piece, and all that she painted was sold except for one portrait, both of which she kept for herself.

At the end of six months she had to have the operation and try for that 2 per cent chance of survival. The night before the operation she decided to make the 'ultimate sacrifice'. The appropriate papers were signed – she donated every one of her organs to those who would live if she lost her race with destiny.

Linda's operation was fatal. But subsequently, her eyes went to a Boston eye bank where a young man, also aged twenty-eight, magically went from darkness to light. He was so profoundly grateful that he wrote to the eye bank with a request to meet and thank the parents of the donor. After pulling many strings and cutting much red tape he was given the name and address of the Birdish family on Staten Island, New York.

He knocked on their door and after hearing his introduction Mrs Birdish hugged him to her bosom and said, 'Young man, if you've got nowhere to go, we would love you to spend the weekend with us.' He stayed.

The next morning as he looked around Linda's room he saw that she'd read Plato as he had read Plato in Braille. She'd read Hegel, as he'd read Hegel in Braille, and the room radiated a cocoon of love and warmth he'd never felt before.

Sunday morning at breakfast, Mrs Birdish was looking at him and said, 'You know, I've seen you somewhere before, but I don't know where.' Then suddenly some 'inner knowledge' triggered within her and she ran upstairs and pulled out the painting Linda had kept aside.

It was a picture of her ideal partner – a portrait of the young man sitting downstairs. Pinned behind it was the last poem that had not been published:

> Yes, I love thee so dearly,
> Words but faintly can express.
> This fond heart beats too sincerely,

Ever in life to love thee less.
So I give to you, dear heart, in passing,
Fleetingly through the night,
A gift of my love everlasting.
But alas! Never to have you in my sight.

Ted Mackness

A NOTE FROM TED MACKNESS: This is my own retelling of what I believe to be a true story. It took place in America and was first reported there on the television program 20/20.

Don't wait until you 'have the time' –
express the 'real' you now.

TURN YOUR
LIFE AROUND

In early 1995 I made a decision I had been stalling on for at least half of my 'forty-something' years – I quit my comfortable salaried position in advertising and marketing and dropped out – or should I say 'dropped in'? It wasn't as if I didn't need the money – the physical me certainly did – it was just that the spiritual Shanks needed something more, something completely different.

I have always wanted to write. In fact, I have always written, but for the last ten or fifteen years, my writing has been almost exclusively related to advertising and marketing. I have won the gongs and the certificates for my work, but it wasn't what I wanted to be writing – I needed a change.

During 1993–94, I completed one book (*A Long Goodnight*, the story of New Zealand's most famous case of euthanasia) but it was a struggle. I would get up at five-thirty every morning and work on the manuscript until nine before changing hats to become

'Mr Ad Man'. At the close of the day's play I would again change hats and fill my evenings (and weekends) working on the book. I was in a perpetual state of exhaustion and my long-suffering wife was married to a man she seldom saw.

A Long Goodnight was published in late 1994, and shortly after it came out, I was approached by a woman named Jan Turner. Jan had read my book and wondered if I would be prepared to help her with her story. I almost said no, but couldn't – it was a tale that deserved to be told.

In early 1995 I finally said yes to Jan. Then, unable to face the prospect of another year constantly changing hats, I made the decision to quit advertising and commit myself to her story. I was forty-six at the time. I knew that unless I made a commitment to change my life at this point, I would go to my grave wondering if I could have done it – if I could have made the break.

Heart-in-mouth, I stepped out into the wilderness and I discovered a strange thing about myself almost immediately. A classic Taurean, I have always had a thing about security, money and possessions. Suddenly, there I was, not knowing where the next buck was coming from. Rather than being overwhelmed by fear and insecurity, I experienced a peculiar sense of freedom that really was quite incredible.

Because I had (and have) a loving and supportive wife at my side, I was secure in myself and my relationship. There was just enough money coming in from my freelance work to pay my way, but no more. It was then that I realised that the material side of things simply didn't matter to me. I was doing what I wanted and I was helping someone tell a story of struggle, hope and survival.

I spent the remainder of 1995 working on the manuscript, which was completed late in the year. I sent it to a publisher a week or so before Christmas and didn't necessarily expect it to be picked up. In the back of my mind was the prospect of the manuscript doing the rounds of the publishing houses and me papering my study walls with rejection slips. But that wasn't a worry. I had completed Jan's story, and that was what really counted. Then, a couple of days before Christmas, I received a call: 'Congratulations. We would like to publish!' What a Christmas present! What a way to end the year!

The book, *We Just Want Our Daughter to Live!*, co-authored with Jan Turner, was released in July 1996. I have already begun work on another book, which also led from Jan's story in the same way that Jan's had followed on from the first book. It seems I am destined to help other people tell their tales, but I don't mind. I am writing what I want to write. There's not a lot of money in it, but there is an enormous sense of satisfaction. There is even time to tinker with a little fiction.

People say that these days I am more relaxed than they could ever remember me being. I look younger than I did a few years ago. I get time to fish while I think on the riverbank. My wife comes home to a ready-cooked dinner and we share our time together well. Another bonus is the fact that I only have to wear one hat.

My advice to others reading this is to go out there and do the thing you have your heart set on before it is too late. Don't be frightened by the prospect of failure – just do it for the soul. To die not reaching your heart's desire would be very sad indeed. I know many who have gone that way. It can't happen to me now – don't let it happen to you!

Grant Shanks

Let go of your attachment to 'security' and
embrace a life of infinite possibility.

TAKING ACTION

CHANGING PRIORITIES

Use this Action Planner to turn the messages in this

chapter into reality in your life. Turn to pages xvi–xvii to

learn the six simple steps you need to know to make the

most of this Action Planner and to enhance your life.

ACTION STEP

Write each of the following on a separate piece of paper:
'health', 'recreation', 'spiritual growth', 'employment/income',
'family/relationships'. Shuffle the pieces around until you have
put them in order of importance in your life.
Write the order down and keep it with you.

MY SPECIFIC ACTION STEP

....

....

....

....

ACTION STEP

The next time you make a major decision, consider
how it will affect the order of your priorities – look
at the list you made in the action step above.

MY SPECIFIC ACTION STEP

....

....

....

....

....

....

ACTION STEP

Write your own obituary. What would you want people to write about you or truthfully say about you at your funeral? Is that how you are living your life now? If not, it's time to change.

MY SPECIFIC ACTION STEP

....

....

....

....

....

....

ACTION STEP

Assume you were told you only had six months to live. Write down the three things you would want to achieve in that time. If you aren't pursuing them now, start planning to.

MY SPECIFIC ACTION STEP

....

....

....

....

....

....

ACTION STEP

Make a 'timetable' of your daily activities over a week.
Does the time spent on each activity reflect your real priorities?
(How much time have you given your partner?
Your children? Your health?)

MY SPECIFIC ACTION STEP

....

....

....

....

....

ACTION STEP

Consult the timetable you made in the previous step.
Find just one activity you can change or eliminate to
allow you more time for your real priorities.

MY SPECIFIC ACTION STEP

....

....

....

....

....

ACTION STEP

Get away. Take at least an hour and go to a quiet place you enjoy. Contemplate your priorities. Are you happy with every aspect of your life? If not, what can you do to change your life and achieve the happiness you deserve?

MY SPECIFIC ACTION STEP

....

....

....

....

....

ACTION STEP

No matter how busy you may be, take time out to exercise – a workout will renew your energy. Go for a walk, a swim, or play a game of squash. Your mind is only as healthy as your body.

MY SPECIFIC ACTION STEP

....

....

....

....

....

LOVING
LIFE

In the noisy confusion of life,
keep peace with your soul.
With all its sham, drudgery
and broken dreams, it is
still a beautiful world.

MY LESSON
IN LIFE

My brother-in-law Des Clarke – a strong, 54-year-old with a wife and seven children to support – was suddenly diagnosed with a malignant brain tumour. During his hospitalisation, every effort was made by his family and friends to give him as much comfort and love as possible.

On one particular evening when my wife and I had planned a visit, I was caught up as usual in 'very important' meetings and arrived at the hospital a few minutes before visiting hours were over.

I apologised profusely for being late and proceeded to describe in boring detail my hectic schedule for the day, including a couple of very serious complaints about the dreadful weather and the impossible traffic.

When I had finished my excuses, Des looked at me with tears in his eyes and said, 'John, you lucky thing.'

He died the following morning.

John Haddad

A NOTE FROM SUE AND DANIEL: When John gave us this piece for the book, he said, 'I've been through a lot in life, I've achieved a lot, but nothing has changed my life more than Des's words.'

Be thankful for the simple things in life.

WINDS OF
CHANGE

It was Christmas Eve. People were rushing around doing their last-minute Christmas shopping, preparing the stuffing for the turkey and enjoying their office parties. All the boys and girls of the city were eagerly awaiting a visit from Santa. They did not know that a different visitor was planning to drop by; a visitor that would turn their lives upside down, shatter their joy, and give them a Christmas they could never forget.

By late afternoon the light sea breeze we'd been enjoying all day had become quite strong so I switched on the radio in the hope of catching the weather report on the four o'clock news. As the radio sprang to life I heard the familiar sound of the cyclone warnings. At this time of year these were a regular occurrence; in fact most people had become quite blasé about them. As day stretched into evening, the storm began to build. The wind was so strong it was forcing the rainwater in between the locked louvre windows and water was running down on to the floor. It occurred to me that I'd have a bit of cleaning up to do before we went out the next day for Christmas dinner. We decided to fill the bath with water and secure the louvred windows with masking tape as the usual cyclone warnings suggested – just in case.

As the evening wore on, I became really frightened. I couldn't even hear the thunder or the driving rain on the tin roof for the roar of the wind. As the storm worsened, we gathered up our baby son and moved into the bathroom. But we were only there for a short time before there was an incredible gust of wind and the sound of twisting metal as the wind picked up our swimming pool, water and all, and tossed it aside like a scrap of paper.

Suddenly there was another terrifying gust and the house shook violently. We tentatively opened the bathroom door and shone the torch up the hallway towards the bedrooms – the torch beam found only a gaping hole. We realised immediately that our house was about to break apart and that we had to find shelter. As we made our way towards the door the louvres imploded and I will never forget the sight of our furniture hurtling towards us across the polished floorboards.

It took all our strength to force the front door open. As we stepped out onto our porch, a gust of wind suddenly lifted my arms in which I was holding our baby son. As my arms and baby went skyward, my husband's hands shot out and grabbed our son before he was torn from me. Against incredible odds, we made our way to our neighbours' house. But our new-found security was short-lived: the storm unleashed more of its fury, ripping our neighbours' kitchen away, and we were on the move again.

We made our way downstairs to the concrete-block toolshed under the house and sat there, huddled together on the floor.

Numb with fear, I watched the entire floor of the house above us lift and crash down repeatedly, and the brick wall itself flex in and out. Eventually, the wall collapsed. There was only one place left to go.

Our neighbours' car was parked under what was left of their house, so we all scrambled in. There we sat, under the debris of their home, for the next four hours waiting and praying. As the storm's fury continued, I wondered whether we'd survive that terrible night.

Cyclone Tracy – the worst cyclone in Australia's recorded history – was a storm of unparalleled ferocity. We lost everything we owned that night, but we were among the lucky ones. Over sixty people lost their lives in Darwin on 24 December 1974. It wasn't our time.

I learnt an incredible lesson that night. Cyclone Tracy taught me how easily life can be snatched away from us and how important it is that we make the most of every moment. It taught me not only to live life to the limit, but to do it *now*. After all, 'now' is all we have. We don't know what the future will hold. We don't even know what the next ten minutes has in store for us. In the words of the late Michael Landon:

> Someone should tell us, right at the start of our lives, that
> we are dying. Then we might live life to the limit, every
> minute of every day. Do it! I say. Whatever you want to
> do, do it now. There are only so many tomorrows.

Jo Wilson

*There may not be a tomorrow so
make the most of today!*

LIFE IS FOR
LIVING

'Life is for living!' I was listening to Florence Houghton (aged eighty-three), who had been talking to me for over an hour, and I was still hanging off every word. She told me she had recently made a tandem parachute jump (the oldest person to do so in the Southern Hemisphere) and was looking forward to her next adventure. However, she was a bit peeved at the backlash she'd received after appearing in a special TV segment.

She had been filmed doing her ordinary supermarket shopping and some 'old fogies' (as she called them) had complained that Florence should not have allowed them to film her putting her 'personals' (like toilet paper) in the trolley. She exclaimed, 'Have they nothing better to notice in life? Must they only criticise? Why do they, when there is so much to see and do of wonder?

'For instance, have you ever seen a spider spin its web? You can sit all day and watch as she creates nature's most magnificent architectural achievement. And then comes the best part,' she sat back and paused dramatically, 'the next morning you get up at dawn and stare in awe at the sight of the dew sparkling on the gossamer threads.' Her eyes blazed with passion as she declared, 'Don't give me diamonds. Just give me dew drops on a spider's web!'

Not surprisingly, Florence and I struck up a great friendship. At the time, I was presenting a talk called 'Young at Heart' for elderly folk, and invited Florence to come and make a brief statement at one of the talks. Well, the audience loved her; Florence completely took over! She told them her six 'L' secrets of life: living, loving, laughing, looking, listening and learning.

Florence says, 'It's easy to really look, and it's so rewarding – if you have the patience.

'Have you ever watched a rosebud bloom? I have. I watched all afternoon as each petal unfolded, one by one, just for me. It was truly beautiful.' Then, with her disarmingly wicked sense of humour, Florence continued: 'Have you ever watched a dandelion bloom? Well, it's like this – you watch and you wait and you watch, and just when you look away to scratch your nose the rotten thing opens!'

With her fierce sense of independence, Florence lives as full a life as she can. Her body is becoming more and more of a challenge but she always trivialises her limitations and turns them into inspirational opportunities. For instance, she calls her walking frame her 'chariot of fire'! She takes every opportunity to speak and will travel anywhere at minimal notice. She fills her life with challenges and thrills, nothing is too difficult: a hot-air balloon ride, a camel ride or a Grand Prix lap with Peter Brock.

Florence Houghton doesn't care that she's a living legend. She only cares about living life to its fullest and inspiring as many hearts as she can to share her passion for appreciating life's every breath.

Thank you, Florence, for your inspiration!

Dr Janet Hall

*Live every moment and appreciate it
for what it is.*

WHEN

'When'. It's only a little word, but use it enough and you'll wake up one day and find that you've missed most of your life.

The problem with 'when' is that it creeps into your thinking. Just the other morning I woke up early and went outside to take in the fresh morning air. A few metres past the clothesline is a rainforest garden we've been trying to establish for some years. The automatic sprinklers had been hard at work, and the dripping leaves of the half-grown trees were glistening as the early morning sun turned them gold. Can you believe what I said to myself? 'The garden is starting to look good. It will be really beautiful in a couple of years.'

Then I went inside and touched my eldest child Mark on the shoulder to wake him up. That's all you have to do to get Mark up and going – the younger two, James and Elizabeth, require much more effort. (Fortunately, the family dog is always happy to lick them awake when all else fails!) Poor Mark was going through what I suffered at his age: acne. Red welts were all over his face, and some had even gone halfway down his back. As I sat on his bed watching him stir, I did it again. I thought, 'Mark, you'll be a handsome man one day.'

Suddenly the enormity of what I'd been thinking hit me. None of us has any guarantees that there will be another day. Just within the last two months, the son of a close friend had been killed in a light plane crash, a 21-year-old nephew had died from a brain haemorrhage, and a twenty-year-old family friend had narrowly escaped death after falling off a building. He was still in a coma. That's why the word 'when' is so dangerous. It robs us of the joy of the moment. You see, the rainforest garden is beautiful now, and it was beautiful when it comprised nothing more than young plants fighting to get established. Mark was a beautiful baby, and he's blossomed into a beautiful teenager.

Everything around us is beautiful – right now.

Noel Whittaker

Experience the joy of the moment.

WHEN I WHINE

The other day upon a bus,
I saw a girl with golden hair.
I envied her, she looked so gay,
And wished I were so fair.
Then suddenly she rose to leave,
I watched her hobble down the aisle.
She had but one leg, and bore a crutch,
And as she passed, a smile.

Oh God forgive me when I whine;
I have two legs, the world is mine!

Later, I paused to buy some sweets.
The lad who sold them had such charm,
I stayed and talked to him a while,

If I were late, 'twould be no harm.
Then as I turned to leave he said,
'Thank you, you have been so kind,
I like to talk with folks like you,
You see, I'm blind.'

Oh God forgive me when I whine;
I have two eyes, the world is mine!

Still later passing down the street,
I saw a child with eyes of blue,
He stood and watched the others play,
It seemed he knew not what to do.
I stood awhile and then I said,
'Why don't you join the others, dear?'
He looked ahead without a word
and then I knew he could not hear.

Oh God forgive me when I whine;
I have two ears, the world is mine!
Two legs to take me where I go,
Two eyes to see the sunset's glow,
Two ears to hear what I would know.
Oh God forgive me when I whine;
I'm blessed indeed, the world is mine.

Author unknown
Submitted by Peter Hornhardt

A NOTE FROM PETER: The author of this poem is unknown. It was given to my mother about thirty years ago and she lovingly used it to deal with her son (me) when he suffered from self-pity. It has stayed with me, despite its archaic and quaint language, and remains a source of inspiration.

A NOTE FROM SUE AND DANIEL: Peter gave us this poem typed on a tattered and faded piece of paper. He'd obviously kept it in his wallet for many years.

Avoid self-pity – focus your thoughts
and energies on what you can achieve.

LIVING FREE

If I could live my life all over again, I'd make more mistakes. I would relax. I would limber up. I would be sillier and crazier than I have been this trip. I would take very few things seriously. I'd laugh more and cry less. I wouldn't worry about what other people thought of me. I would accept myself as I am. I would climb more mountains, swim more rivers and watch more sunsets. I would eat more ice-cream and less beans. I would have more picnics and watch less TV. I would feel only sad, not depressed; concerned, not anxious; annoyed, not angry. I would regret my mistakes but not feel guilty about them.

I would tell more people that I liked them. I would hug my friends. I would forgive others for being human and hold no grudges. I would play with more children and listen to more old people. I would go after what I wanted without believing I needed it and place less value on money.

You see, I am one of those people who live cautiously and sensibly and sanely, hour after hour, day after day. Oh, I've had my moments, and if I had my time over again, I'd have more of them. In fact, I'd have nothing else – just moments, one after another, instead of living so many years ahead of each day. I've been one of those people who never goes anywhere without a thermometer, a hot-water bottle, a raincoat and a parachute. If I could do it over again I would travel lighter.

I would start barefoot earlier in the spring and stay that way till after the autumn. I would go to more dances. I wouldn't get such good marks (except by accident). I would ride more merry-go-rounds. I'd pick more daisies and smile more because I'd be living free.

Author unknown
Submitted by **Barbara Pettigrew**

A NOTE FROM SUE AND DANIEL: This is a well-known piece which can be found in many forms. It is often attributed to an 85-year-old woman from Kentucky.

Set yourself free – enjoy the magic
of each moment.

I'M HAPPY
HERE

Like most young people, the thought of my mother dying terrified me. She told me firmly that there was nothing to be afraid of and that I'd be amazed at how peaceful the whole thing would be. I couldn't take her words in. She and I were so vital then. Thirty-plus years on, I tested her words. To me, my mother was always a magical kind of person; not ordinary like the rest of us. How else, I wondered, could she so lovingly and powerfully have affected the lives of so many others when her own personal life was unbelievably difficult?

A wisp of a woman, she ate like a bird yet had the heart and energy of a lion. Constantly on the move, she reminded you of the 'tw' in twinkle, the fizz and crack of a flame. Watching her living out her final weeks both captivated and humbled me. She taught me the meaning of courage, tenacity, joy and love.

With only days to live, my mother was being shunted

around the hospital. We tracked her down that Wednesday, in a new ward. Her view from the window was no longer of a beautiful garden; instead, just brick walls. Frustrated and annoyed that she'd been moved I told her I'd get her shifted back, or at least moved to a better position. 'Oh, no Hen [my pet name],' she said, 'those are the walls of the Geelong Prison. They help me to think of the poor young boys in there. Those walls make me glad your four brothers aren't in trouble, and being here helps me to pray better for those who're suffering inside.'

Pearl Sumner

Be thankful for all that you have.

DIGGING MY
HEELS IN

Throughout my life I have tried to avoid situations 'getting the better of me' and have been able to put trials and tribulations into perspective. Perhaps this has been easier for me, being a child during the Second World War.

For most of my adult life I worked hard, played hard, made money, lost money, enjoyed many successes and suffered failures. It was all fun and a challenge and I enjoyed the trappings of being a businesswoman: the regular overseas trips, collecting antiques, driving fast cars, entertaining in style, and being seen at the right place at the right time. During those heady days there was little time to take stock, or to contemplate the meaning of life.

It was in my late thirties that I achieved my greatest success, my son Angus. The break-up of my marriage early in the piece made me determined to be a great mum, and to nurture my son into becoming a happy, well-adjusted, compassionate and respected human being.

It was when Angus was thirteen that I first became ill, displaying tiredness and dizziness, lethargy and some other very distressing symptoms. I stayed home more and more but sought continual medical advice, had numerous tests and was virtually told it was in my mind – a combination of menopause and stress.

After two and a half years of anguish it was almost a relief when I was diagnosed with cancer. Clearly, something *had* been terribly wrong. I had felt my body was dying; it was not 'all in my mind'. My first reaction was to race home, pour a glass of wine and cuddle my enormous old almond tree which was about to burst into blossom. (In retrospect, it never bloomed that year; instead, I believe, gave me its energy to help me confront the challenges that lay ahead.)

The panic buttons hit and my specialists acted quickly. Massive surgery proved that a rare cancer was invading my body and had spread to my ovaries and liver. It is a cancer that is reasonably slow moving, but still tenacious. It is considered incurable and untreatable; in short, terminal.

Suddenly life's odds were against me and I had to learn to live with it. I had to learn to live with the chronic pain and the distressing symptoms, with watching my body waste and deteriorate. I was determined to be productive and positive, and to focus my mind on leading as normal a life as possible.

Having cancer is more than a full-time job – it is impossible to forget, even for a moment, that you have it, but outwardly to friends and family you have to learn to be a wonderful and convincing actor. You experience a whole range of emotions: hope, despair, sadness, disbelief and eventually some happiness (which can only come with a sense of acceptance and a deepening spirituality). The truly simple pleasures of life become dominant: colours seem more beautiful, a friend's smile creates an inner joy, there is time for contemplation and visualisation, time for prayer and meditation, time to experience true quality.

Eighteen months ago I instigated a new life. My son (now seventeen) and I moved to the Gold Coast and I firmly believe this has given me more time. My days are still dictated by painkillers, including morphine, plus injections. I have learnt to self-administer, and am now energetic enough to assist in raising funds for the Queensland Cancer Fund. I have been in and out of palliative care, I have regular blood tests, scans, abdominal drainage treatment, doctor and specialist visits – each an ordeal.

My son Angus is achieving at school and in surf lifesaving and kayaking; we're both aiming for the Sydney Olympics. He is my inspiration. I'm too much of a 'sticky beak' not to want to be around to see him become an even finer young man. He has shown resolute strength and faith when I have been close to death, he has given me the power to battle the odds, he has helped me accept myself for what I now am – hopefully a better and more understanding person.

Frequently I feel reclusive and need to be alone. In these times I have taken up collecting and creating bonsai and I can care for and communicate with these miniature trees and plants. I'm trying to propagate an almond tree, just to remind me that nature is ever so much more powerful than we are and that we must respect this.

I have never thought 'why me'. I just believe I'm one of the unlucky statistics. There are many answers to be found, particularly now that the disease has become so prevalent, and while research is achieving results in many areas, awareness and early detection is vital. I can only advise others to listen to their body, minimise anxiety and stress, lead a moderate life, exercise regularly without going overboard, and cut down on the use of chemicals and electrical appliances. Most cancers take time to develop; some are preventable, some take the form of obvious lumps, while others just grow and grow unseen and unfelt for years. The rare ones, such as mine, are also hard to diagnose and any answer seems better than none. However, in my experience, acceptance and complacency should not be on the agenda. Seek answers (get second or third opinions if necessary); the truth, however hard, at least allows us the opportunity to develop that fighting spirit and mental strength that we all have but rarely show. Expel those in your life that drain you of your precious energy, fill your life with unconditional love, make time to marvel at the simple pleasures: take a barefoot stroll along the beach, a walk through the fresh mountain air, listen to the birds courting and flirting, watch the sky at dawn, feel the stillness of a sunset.

Create new challenges, learn new skills, paint new pictures, enjoy each and every minute, be gentle, take a deep breath and be thankful for what you have. Above all, stay healthy – it is the greatest gift of all.

Jennie Ham Washington

A NOTE FROM SUE: Sadly, my friend Jennie passed away, but she will always have a place in my heart.

Live every day to its fullest.

A Meeting in
New York

A few years ago I was lucky enough to have spent two weeks in one of my favourite places in the world – Aspen. I was enjoying myself so much that on the final day I took the last possible flight to Denver and connection to New York.

    I arrived in New York very late. There were no taxis available so I took a bus into the Port Authority bus station at West 33rd Street. As I struggled with my two suitcases – carrying them alternately as they were too heavy to carry simultaneously – one of the passengers offered to help, suggesting that this was not the time or place for a woman to be on her own. He kindly helped me to a taxi and I was driven to a small hotel at 54th and Madison.

    It was only after the taxi drove off that I realised the hotel was locked and I was alone on the street at two o'clock in the morning in Manhattan. I started banging on the windows and finally woke the night porter who took me to my room. As grateful as I was to be off the street, the room looked to my Australian eyes like an inside-out prison cell with all the locks on the inside! My Aspen high was beginning to subside.

Next morning at around ten o'clock I went walking down Madison Avenue. As I wandered along in a dream, two very large men came up beside me, one on each side like two bodyguards.

Because of my Aspen state of mind, I did not have my normal 'wary traveller' guards up (handbag under coat et cetera). Instead, my shoulder bag was outside my jacket. Suddenly it felt much lighter. I looked down to see the flap open and my wallet gone. The two men were still on either side of me. I kept walking and looked from one to the other, realising that one of them had my wallet. I turned to the man closest to my bag and said, 'Excuse me, I have just lost my wallet. I am an Australian travelling alone and my wallet has everything I need – my passport, credit cards, airline ticket and money.' The man looked at me and handed me back my wallet! I thanked him and the two walked off.

A woman came up to me and told me she had seen everything from behind. She said she was as stunned as I that he had given it back to me. She left and I stood alone, shaking, in the street.

To this day I am unsure if it was my Australian accent, the sheer honesty of my request, or the calm (stunned!), polite way I asked for the wallet. Perhaps some people in the world have never been treated as if they are capable of honesty, or even politeness!

Marcia Griffin

Appeal to the 'goodness' in everyone
you encounter.

LEARN TO LOVE

You're here to learn to love, that's what life is all about.
You're here to learn to love, so you should never doubt.
All your dreams are possible, all your thoughts are real.
You're born to learn the lessons that the mind will soon reveal.

When you learn to love, you create such magic dreams.
When you learn to love, you'll discover wondrous schemes;
Ways to achieve the possible, ways to achieve your aims,
The universe can give you all you wish for, all you claim.

When you really learn to love, you'll discover magic powers;
Ways to live a life that's full with many happy hours.
Everything you long for will surely come your way,
For love just guarantees success for each and every day.

Go share your love with everyone. It's free, it can't be bought.
It's only when you give it that its value will be sought
By those who never had it, till you gave them some to share,
And then your love will blossom as your gift grows everywhere.

So learn to love your neighbours, love everyone you meet.
The human race is precious, creation's greatest feat.
Do not be judgemental, you're here to learn it's true
That love's the only power that can ever conquer you.

Jack Hone

Love is the greatest gift
you have to offer –
give it freely.

THE MOST
MEANINGFUL CALL

Some couples openly express their love for one another by hugging, kissing and saying 'I love you' openly to each other and their children. Graham and I did not have that sort of a family. We had a home filled with love and five beautiful children, but we just weren't the expressive type.

Then one day it came time to talk about love – I needed to reassure my daughter how much I loved her and how much her father had loved her before he passed away. You see, my daughter was dying of cancer. In those last few months when I would sit at her bedside and simply say, 'I love you', I could see a twinkle in her eye. It meant so much to her to hear those words.

I was at her bedside one day when the phone rang. It was her brother-in-law Nathan and his two children, Ashley and Tyler. Bubbling with enthusiasm and energy Nathan said, 'Can I speak with Linda?' I tried to explain that she was absolutely exhausted and didn't even have the energy to hold the phone, but he begged me to place the phone next to her ear on the pillow. So that's exactly what I did.

Nathan and his children did not speak to Linda, they sang instead. It was the words to Stevie Wonder's song 'I Just Called to Say I Love You'; they had been practising for several days. When they finished, Linda's face filled with the radiant joy of knowing how much someone loves you. With all the strength she could muster she murmured, 'That's so beautiful.'

Linda died three days later, but not before knowing she was accepted, appreciated and loved in this life.

Yvonne Clifton

Tell someone you love them;
it is a priceless gift.

THE LAMPLIGHTER

My mother-in-law, Scotty, would sometimes tell me stories about her childhood in Glasgow. She once told me of the old lamplighter who was known as the 'Leery'. Every evening at dusk the old man would move down the street with a long pole which had a tiny flame at the end of it, lighting one lamp after another, bringing light to the whole district.

Scotty ended her story with the remark, 'After a while, son, the Leery would be completely out of sight, way down the street somewhere. But you could always tell which way he'd gone by the light he left behind.'

Peter Sumner

Leave everyone you touch feeling a little brighter.

HOME BASE

I always tell my parents that I love their white hair, though sometimes I wonder if I'm responsible for most of it! Always the easy-going second child, I seem to have made up for my placid childhood with a series of incidents in my adult life. The first was a motor accident resulting in a broken spine and broken legs and, a year later, one of Australia's first spinal fusions (successful, thank heavens!).

Mum and Dad, the eternal optimists, believed in my total recovery and that I would regain a full life. They helped me in so many ways during my year in a wheelchair and brace. Perhaps most importantly, they helped me to laugh – like the time my legs were in plaster and I wanted a bath. The only way we could get me in the bath was with my legs resting on buckets, which was fine until we let the water out and I got stuck. We laughed so much I was incapable of helping myself out.

Later they loved and supported me through the death of my fiancee. I went overseas to try to get my life together and their hilarious letters followed me all over the world. On my way home, I managed to trick them into believing I was still in England, then I arrived home to surprise them both on Mum's birthday. The rest of the family were worried that one of them might keel over with the shock. Not likely! It was a noisy, rambunctious night!

When I first moved to Melbourne, they made regular trips, often with a tool box and drill, to help me settle into my new home. During my six years there, the breakdown of a very special relationship took me a long time to get over. My mum encouraged me to meet with my ex-lover and say goodbye properly and in so doing I was able to let go and get on with my life. Later, I met my husband and we moved back to Adelaide to start a business together. However, it was a disaster, and after seven years the marriage failed and I went home to Mum and Dad – more white hairs.

Eventually I found a new career in Canberra. My life was very successful, very busy and very demanding. I included Mum and Dad wherever I could, taking them overseas and bringing them to Canberra as often as I was able.

After four and a half years, and a particularly difficult time, I left Canberra and moved to Melbourne. It seemed my life was changing around me and I was no longer in control of my future. Mum and Dad were there again, as always, supportive and loving.

Finally, my own business is taking off and I am learning not to make my job the focus of my life. My wonderful parents are still there and have taught me so much. They've taught me about unconditional love – to be there for someone, no matter what the circumstances, and remain steadfast in your belief in the person you love.

Elizabeth Boydell

*Be there, no matter what,
to support those you love.*

HEIDI

I had never had a pet. I was also the younger of two children, so I never learnt to care for someone else. At twenty-seven I bought my wife a German shepherd puppy for protection because I travelled a lot and we had just had our first child. It was a tough learning experience.

Heidi always loved me unconditionally. If I growled at her for chewing something up or wetting the floor, she would still come back, head and tail down, for reconciliation. I came to love her and she became my dog. When no one else would talk to me, she would sidle up, lick my hand and bump my leg for a pat. We went through a lot together.

With three children, part-time study, renovating houses, a tough job and trying to stay happily married, life was never dull. We walked every day for about thirteen years, out in the cold or heat, always mates. I fed her, trained her, loved her and, eventually, buried her. At thirteen she had arthritis and couldn't walk. My wife and I took her to the vet, and held her as that awful green liquid took her life. We had a funeral service. I dug the hole. We all said a few words, then I laid Heidi to rest. Never thought I'd love a dog, but I did, I do, and I will again.

Murray Hine

Learn to love, it is the most
powerful force on earth.

TAKING ACTION

LOVING LIFE

❧

Use this Action Planner to turn the messages in this

chapter into reality in your life. Turn to pages xvi–xvii to

learn the six simple steps you need to know to make the

most of this Action Planner and to enhance your life.

ACTION STEP

Write down all the reasons why you feel
fortunate – re-read the list and add to it
from time to time.

MY SPECIFIC ACTION STEP

....

....

....

....

....

....

ACTION STEP

Write to a parent or guardian
thanking them for something positive
they taught you.

MY SPECIFIC ACTION STEP

....

....

....

....

....

....

ACTION STEP

Create your own positive affirmation
reminding you how beautiful life is. Record it and
listen to it when you are feeling down.

MY SPECIFIC ACTION STEP

....
....
....
....
....
....

ACTION STEP

When you are at a standstill in traffic or waiting at a red light,
release your grip on the steering wheel and feel a wave of
relaxation travel through your body.

MY SPECIFIC ACTION STEP

....
....
....
....
....
....

ACTION STEP

Stop. Make the time to stroll through a park, to listen to a
bird call, to watch the sun set, to inhale the perfume of a
flower . . . just once, for a moment or two, every day.

MY SPECIFIC ACTION STEP

....

....

....

....

....

....

ACTION STEP

Whenever you see your reflection give yourself a
'check-up from the neck up' and put a smile on your face.
It costs nothing and brightens up the day.

MY SPECIFIC ACTION STEP

....

....

....

....

....

....

LEARNING FROM LIFE

*Take kindly the counsel of the years,
gracefully surrendering the
things of youth.*

PRECIOUS LIFE

When I was a young boy my parents used to take me to one of Victoria's most popular old tourist towns for at least one of the school holidays each year. The township is called Warburton.

My mother and I would stay at the Warburton Chalet (a famous guesthouse at the time; it has since burned down) and my father would join us each weekend after working in Melbourne during the week. The Warburton Chalet was owned by an uncle of mine, Jules Mayer, and was set in the beautiful Warburton Valley at the foot of Mount Little Joe. Warburton itself, as I remember, was a magical place sprinkled with tall eucalypts, elms and oak trees. The Yarra River flows through the town and along its banks grew ferns, willows and poplar trees.

One Saturday morning when my father was up for the weekend, we decided to go on one of the chalet's organised walks. We headed off through fern gullies and over small crystal-clear streams in the hills near the chalet. There were about eight of us on the walk enjoying the peace and fresh air of the Australian bush. Along the way our guide would point out things of interest such as birds, spiders, lizards, shrubs and the like.

We soon came to the 'Fruit Salad Farm'. This unusual place was a favourite in the area and had an odd assortment of garden statues, metal arches overgrown with vines and a wild garden filled with native bush. You felt like you were in another land. The Fruit Salad Farm served up – you guessed it – fruit salad and ice-cream. It was a special place, a place where you could get lost in your own imagination. How fortunate we were to be able to visit it!

We then continued on our journey up the hillside and came upon a small clearing in the bush. The clearing was actually a farm and on that farm was the most amazing sight I had ever seen – thousands and thousands of white geese contrasting against the velvet green of the lush grass. None of the group had ever seen anything like it before.

Sitting on a log beside a fence was an old man with a distinctive red beret on his head. He had a weather-beaten face and a broad smile. He was pleased to see us and asked us what we were all up to. It was hard not to notice that behind this old man's smile lay a line of broken and stumpy teeth. When he raised his hands to light his pipe, I also noticed he was missing a number of fingers. While time had certainly taken its toll on this man's face, conspicuous scars penetrated his cheeks, forehead and the backs of his hands.

One of our group asked why there were so many geese. The old man's eyes filled with tears and he told us his story, a story that stays with me to this day, some thirty years on.

He was from Poland: 'A small village in a beautiful valley,

very much like this one. I was a young man then, full of hope and
life, with plenty to look forward to. But then war broke out and
many Poles were captured by the Germans and put into concentration camps.'

He said he remembered asking what he had done wrong.
'For this I had my index finger cut off. I soon learnt not to ask many
questions from then on.

'Months and years went by. The only thing that kept me
alive was hope and the thoughts of seeing my family and young
wife again. We had our teeth broken or filed out of our mouths to
obtain the gold fillings. It was done in a most brutal manner. Even
if you had only a couple of teeth filled, about ten others were broken or pulled just to get to them. You were then left in agony with
your mouth and gums bleeding,' he said.

The old man held up a matchbox and told us that this was
about the size of the food ration they were allowed each day. 'Half
the time, it was crawling with maggots,' he said. 'I once stole an
extra food ration and for my trouble had four fingers cut off by one
of the guards. They did it with garden shears.' He showed us his
hand.

'Eventually a number of us mustered enough courage to try
a daring but still foolhardy escape. Some of us made it, many
others did not. It was only after the war that I could start the search
for my family.' The old man paused for some time, then with a
broken voice he slowly continued his story. 'They were all dead.
Tortured, killed or starved to death by the Nazis.' He then turned
and looked at his geese.

'You see,' he said, 'this is why I have so many, many geese.
I eventually moved to Australia and found this little valley, so much
like mine in Poland – peaceful and quiet with so much beauty. I

decided to buy and farm a handful of geese, but when it came time to slaughter one with an axe or with my bare hands, I could not do it. I kept on remembering the camp with all its torture and senseless bloodshed. I could no longer stand the sight of blood or death, no matter what sort of living creature it was. Life is far too precious, you see. So now I have all these geese and I don't know what to do. But I know one thing, I can't bear to see any more bloodshed in my life.'

Our group stood motionless and silent for some time and I remember feeling a very deep sorrow for this old man, something that I had never felt before in my short life. I had not heard stories of the horrors of war and concentration camps before. It made me realise just how lucky I was to live in a place like Australia and how precious life is.

We wished the old man well and continued on our way. I sometimes wonder what has since become of the old man and his geese. His story and our journey that day will remain with me forever. We truly do live a fortunate life.

Mark Thomson

All life is sacred – never take it for granted.

ROLE REVERSAL

My dad is on his last legs. Now eighty-four and quite frail, he's in a nursing home where a caring staff help him achieve the daily tasks he once took for granted: getting in and out of bed, washing, getting dressed, walking.

He's not the man he was and he's the first to admit it. In his prime he was quite a sportsman. He played football and cricket. He competed successfully with the East Melbourne Harriers. He represented Victoria in yachting and lacrosse. As he got older golf became his passion.

Our Sunday roast dinner was inevitably accompanied by Dad's account of his morning golf round – the whole eighteen holes, stroke by stroke. He'd usually finished by the time I was demolishing my second helping of Nan's apple pie and cream. After lunch he'd get stuck into the garden, which usually meant irksome weeding and raking chores for my brother and me. Mum and

Nan would bake scones or shortbread or make a sponge cake. We kids got to scrape the basin – first the cake mix, then the orange icing.

I look at my dad, dozing in his chair by the window, and he's all skin and bones now, his cheeks hollow. Above him on the wall is a photo of a racehorse he once had an interest in.

He wakes up and I clean his eyes and give him the bad news about the once mighty Demons. Together Dad and I had seen all those classic Melbourne–Collingwood clashes of the fifties and sixties. And I think about the way our roles are now reversed and what Dad meant to me when I was a boy growing into a young man.

My dad was a regular bloke. I know he and Mum went without so they could send us kids to a private school. They thought we'd get a better education, and I'm sure we did. He believed in good manners and respect for your elders but he wasn't stuck on undue formality. Even as kids we called all my parents' friends by their first names. He taught us to give up our seats to ladies on trains and trams so it became second nature to us. I still do it, even if people these days sometimes regard me with suspicion.

He insisted, back in the fifties before it was mandatory, that if I was to be a good footballer I had to kick with both feet. It got me out of a lot of trouble. He once told me that if you could read, you could cook. And so now I can cook.

Dad left school at fifteen, joined Pelaco the shirt manufacturers, and spent the rest of his working life in the men's clothing business. Former colleagues tell me he was one of the gentlemen of the industry. He dressed well – his suits were tailored and he always wore a hat – and his word was as good as his bond.

He had a sense of humour and loved his beer with the boys

at the pub on the way home from work. He called England 'Home' and he reckoned Bob Menzies was a champion.

My mum was a whiz at flower arrangements, had a couple of Van Gogh prints on the wall, and in the fifties she took in Thai students and made them part of the family.

In my late teens I became interested in European films, went to art galleries, and was seduced by jazz. The arts was not something Dad was interested in, and there were times I wished he was more worldly, more cosmopolitan. I used to feel very frustrated when we couldn't connect. I decided he was a dead-set square and I saw myself as a real groover. It was the beginning of the generation gap. Our only real common ground was the footy.

He had his ways and that was pretty much that, but I was impatient to broaden my horizons and there were inevitable confrontations. 'Dad, you don't understand!' I used to rail, the same adolescent *cri de coeur* that I have heard from my own son at times. I only began to really appreciate my parents as I approached forty. I stopped trying to change them, influence them, con them. Most important of all, I stopped judging them. I thought back on what I'd put them through as I chased my rainbow, how oblivious I was to their feelings.

Only now can I acknowledge that my confidence and self-esteem grew from the environment of love and security that was my home. My parents often didn't understand me, true, but they gave me a fair go. I was able to have my say and be listened to, even if they didn't agree with my opinions. Sometimes they came down on me like a ton of bricks but generally I was allowed room to move.

Nowadays I'm happy to acknowledge that their values have become my values. I may have developed a vastly different lifestyle but those guiding principles were passed on – the lore of the elders nurturing the next generation. Hopefully I can do the same for my kids.

A long time ago Dad impressed upon me the great virtue of what he called The Golden Rule. 'Do unto others as you would have them do to you.' Such crystal-clear logic! Such common sense! Treat people the way you'd like them to treat you. It was a blueprint for life.

Fourteen years ago I held my mum's hand as her spirit left her, her body racked by cancer. 'I'm a bit of a crook chook,' she'd whispered to me. And now I look at my dad, so vulnerable in his twilight years, and I muse on how men, especially Australian men, find it difficult to physically and verbally express their love for one another.

Dad used to kiss me until, at about thirteen, I rejected it as unmanly. A few years back I started to give him a hug or a kiss when the occasion seemed appropriate. This time round it was his turn to be uncomfortable. Now as I lean over and plant my lips on his shiny scalp he doesn't mind at all.

Thanks for everything, Dad. I love ya!

Rennie Ellis

Tell your parents how much
you appreciate them, today!

My Mum's Wish

I recall that we were free, our spirits wild and adventurous. Pain, except for the odd graze or blackening bruise, was foreign to me. Our family was a unit, bonded by love; as small children we were never denied attention.

My most vivid memories are of the times we were all together. We would often have communal bath times – Mum, tall and slender, and her four children all crammed in the enamel tub together. When my younger brother was unborn we would coat Mum's oversized belly with a thick lather of our special blue soap, and write in huge letters 'Fat Albert'.

When my brother had grown a little he took a fancy to scissors and snipped away his beautiful hair to create his own masterpiece, but Mum could only laugh at the bald patches on his head.

I always remember that if something went wrong, Mum would make it right. We were always woken from our nightmares by the soothing warmth of Mum's voice touching our fear. It was Mum's warm hand against our bare flesh that taught us right from wrong, and guided us to become, as she was, caring, generous, imaginative . . . and brave.

I always believed Mum was going to get better. After all, that was why we took so many trips to doctor's surgeries and hospitals, wasn't it? Of course they were going to fix her. I was never told much about her sickness. I gathered that a growth inside her kept growing, but I thought the doctors would fix it. During this time we still spent a great deal of time together, in or out of hospitals – the same bonded unit of happiness.

I will never forget the day my father said these words: 'There's nothing more the doctors can do.' At first I thought it sounded like great news: no more hospitals, no more pain for Mum and we could move back to our old home, and even go to our old school. But my illusions were shattered with my father's next words: 'Mummy's going to die, darling.' I was nine years old.

Our family was suddenly tormented by emotional heartbreak. We each took the news in our own way, but we all knew that to face reality meant saying goodbye to someone we all loved and depended on. We would all live on with Mum inside us.

It is only by accepting the past, with its pleasure and pain, that I am able to reach for the future and strive for happiness in what I do – for that was Mum's wish.

Eliza Stacey

*Make peace with the past and those you love
will stay with you forever.*

UNREASONABLE
FRIENDS

In 1989 thousands of Australian businesses were thrown into crisis by a national airline dispute which lasted more than six months. Suddenly businesses in this far-flung country had to learn how to get along without air travel. Such a crisis quickly created catastrophic consequences for many businesses; mine was one of them.

My seminar business was a national operation with branches in most states and it relied upon being able to use the airlines almost every day. Overnight everything ground to a halt. Within two months, my twelve-year-old, highly successful business had collapsed. My self-esteem took a nose dive and things got very bad, very quickly. When I thought I'd reached rock bottom, my wife decided that enough was enough and asked me to leave. It was the end of a very special eighteen-year relationship. I was totally devastated!

I started to feel pretty sorry for myself and for months I

went around being depressed and telling my sad story to any of my friends who would listen. Each month my story got sadder and I got even more sympathy from these well-meaning friends.

Then one evening I was in a coffee shop in South Yarra when I met up with an extraordinary person who was to have a major impact on my life. This person introduced themself and explained that they'd attended many of the seminars I had promoted through the eighties.

'What's your next big seminar coming up?' they asked.

I put on my most depressed voice and for the next thirty minutes I explained what had happened. This person sat quietly, expressionless, and after hearing my story asked, 'So what have you done about getting on with your life since then?'

This was not the reaction I was used to. I expected sympathy and understanding, which is what most friends will give you when you are feeling low like this. But the truth is, sympathy rarely helps. Sympathy very often supports us staying exactly where we are. Miserable! Depressed! Uninspired!

This person looked me in the eyes and finally said, 'Wayne, what are you going to do about all of this? What are you going to do to get your life moving again?'

I was almost in shock at their lack of sensitivity. Didn't this person understand how impossible it was for me to change my situation right now? All of my other friends did! I was shaken.

The next morning this person telephoned me and asked, 'So, what are you going to do today to improve your situation? What's your plan?' I said I didn't have a plan and they suggested that I had best get one quick. This person was being so unreasonable with me! Every day this new friend telephoned me and asked the same questions, and every day refused to accept my sad excuses.

Then suddenly it occurred to me that this person was being totally unreasonable with me because they really cared about me! They were prepared to tell me things about myself that most of my friends were not prepared to tell me.

Here's the lesson I learnt: If you really want to grow, surround yourself with friends who expect more of you than you do of yourself – friends who are prepared to be unreasonable with you in your best interests. In other words, friends who care enough to press you out of your 'comfort zone'. I now call friends like this 'unreasonable friends'!

These days I surround myself with many 'unreasonable friends' in both my business and in my personal life. As a consequence I have grown more in the past five years than I had in the previous ten. I've also worked out that the best way to be a real friend to the people I care about most is to tell them the truth too (as I see it) and become their 'unreasonable friend'.

My original 'unreasonable friend' eventually became managing director of my company as it grew and prospered. A couple of years later I married this unreasonable friend and today Wendy McCrum continues to be my most unreasonable friend – my best friend – inspiring me to become more, achieve more, do more. I thank God every day that Wendy came into my life when she did.

Wayne Berry

If you really want to grow,
surround yourself with friends
who expect more of you
than you do of yourself.

284

We Haven't
Got a Daddy
Any More

I was ten years old when my daddy died. His name was Jack, and I guess that sums him up: ordinary, straightforward and unpretentious.

I was seven when he first went into hospital. I don't remember much after that, but what I do recall are very strong feelings of tenderness, and sensations from precious moments.

I can feel his tummy rising and falling as I sit on his lap while he reads his Zane Grey western. I feel loved and secure. I can see him crossing the bedroom floor in his pyjamas by the passage light as he comes to bed. When Mum goes out to a school committee meeting I am allowed to warm her side of the bed alongside Daddy. He starts his poem:

> Pip and Pol went off to sea
> Aboard the Saucy Anne
> With lots of ham and jam and tea,
> A pot and frying pan.

Somewhere around verse sixteen when Pip and Pol are well and truly lost at sea and I have dropped off to sleep, Daddy shakes the bed as he shouts, 'A ship! A ship! Pip one day cried.' I sense he does it on purpose, but I fall back to sleep knowing that he'll finish the poem and get Pip and Pol home without my help.

He knocks on the bedroom wall next morning and I toddle into the bathroom to help him clean and reassemble his safety razor. It's my job. He pays me every Friday night with piles of pennies, 'hape-nees' and 'throopences' from his loose change. He counts it out on the table while my mother scolds him, 'Oh, Jack!'. I don't think he deserves the scolding.

I see him tuned into the Saturday night radio; I'm on the floor at his feet with the cat and Mum is roasting almonds in the fireplace. He mimics the gun sound effects in the detective dramas. He chuckles at the characters in the variety shows.

I see him turning the sods of earth around the nectarine tree 'to air the roots'. I see him by the tank stand stirring blue copper sulphate mix (for curly leaf on the peach tree) in the galvanised iron bucket, using a flat stick to make the whirlpool in the middle. Even today, the sound of a galvanised iron bucket clinking on concrete takes me back to the tank stand alongside him. Tomorrow's children will have so little to remember in the sound of plastic buckets. There's romance in a real bucket.

I see him twirl his hard-boiled egg every morning, leaving me its 'hat' to eat, and leaving me a sip of black tea to drink in the bottom of his cup. 'Sugared?' he asks, every time, as Mum hands him his cup.

I recall a man of consistent and quiet habits. A man of low ambition but high principles. A gentle man; a loving man; a man of kindness and no pretences. He shone his shoes till he could see his face in them. He wore a brown three-piece suit to work and waved goodbye over Bob Michell's hedge as he rounded the corner to catch the tram.

I see him suffering in his hospital bed bathed in perspiration, gasping for breath in his oxygen mask while his heart played its last agonising asynchronous beats in his chest.

I see his blue eyes burning his love into me. I hear the minister say, 'Jack, your wife and little boy will be fine. Leave them in God's care.' He did exactly that. He could have done no better.

I was playing the piano that Sunday night when Mum came in from the hospital. The house was suddenly quiet. My aunt was there. My big brothers were lingering in the passage. My mother sat down alongside me and said, 'You know something's wrong, don't you? We haven't got a daddy any more.'

I ran sobbing to my bed. She followed me. She told me our daddy was in heaven and he had to go because it was the only place that could fix him. He would never know any more suffering. It was for the best.

It seemed logical to me. It made sense. I accepted it. But I was deeply sad and knew a new level of loneliness that has never left me.

It's funny how he's still there in my memory, locked in pictures and impressions. I haven't had a daddy these thirty-eight years, yet in countless ways I have.

Colin Pearce

Cherish your memories –
they are a critical part of you –
then move forward to positively
embrace who you are today.

A Mother's Love

She was born on 1 May 1937 and given the name Elizabeth Lemore Sanger, yet throughout her life, everyone would know her by her nickname – Penny. She was the last child born to her loving parents, Paul and Alice Sanger.

Growing up near the beautiful green forests of Washington, she had many opportunities to experience the true outdoors as a child. Camping and fishing trips near Mount St Helens and Mount Rainer were a regular family pastime.

When World War II came along, her father was a commander in the air force, successfully teaching many young men how to fly B-17s and B-24s to defend their country. His logged air hours for both civilian and military duty would be just over 23 400 by the time he retired in 1969.

During those lonely years when her father was in active service, her mother would be the strong disciplinarian and support for the children. Both her mother and father worked hard to keep family life together and when the war was over, the celebrations went on for months and months. It was a time when family bonds and community ties were strengthened.

As Penny grew older, her passion for education, sports, community involvement and helping others became evident to all who came to know her. In 1954 she was voted by her classmates to be the homecoming queen. The following year, she graduated as the number one student in her class. Her valedictory message (as retold by others later) inspired over 500 of her fellow graduating classmates to hold their heads high, to walk tall as adults and to leave the proud legacy of their accomplishments as a benchmark in their family history.

Forgoing her college education, she spent the next year taking care of her mother, whose ailing health was in the early stages of a non-recoverable heart condition. Within a year she had met her husband, an outstanding football player and rugged outdoors man. They married and had three children within three years. She poured her love out to her family and often told friends that her proudest achievements in life were her three beautiful children.

Through the years, we all loved Penny and she gave so much to so many; she always had a smile and an open ear for friends and family. However, the Christmas of 1972 would prove to be the most difficult period of her life. Earlier that year, she had gone through a very painful operation to remove cancer from her reproductive organs. The operation was a complete success except for one thing. Within weeks of the operation, Penny knew she felt different – weak and not full of the energy she had always had. It would take many tests to find the cause and try to eliminate the effects. The blood transfusions during her operation had transferred the cells of a very rare form of leukemia called aplastic anaemia.

By November 1972 she knew that the chances of her recovery were almost nil. At that time only she, her husband and doctors already knew that this unforgiving, incurable blood disease would eventually take her life. She decided to tell her children the truth and to give them the facts at hand.

She told her children on Christmas Day to always be there for each other, to care and give to each other even when it wasn't easy. She said that they would have to learn adult responsibilities very early and to be patient with one another. Knowing that her words would have to last a lifetime, she chose each of them carefully. She told them to always do the right thing in situations that involved other people and that if they ever had doubts about what was right or wrong, they should ask for guidance through prayer.

She lived well beyond the six months the doctors had predicted. Over the next year and a half she lived one day at a time and, even with all the hospital visits and the agony of the disease, she lived and loved each one of us and gave us new reasons to love each other.

The church service was beautiful. A thousand people gathered inside and another 400 outside to give Penny their respects. More importantly, they each brought with them their love for her and it confirmed that one person can touch so many people in such a short lifetime.

She is remembered by so many people in stories that are retold each Christmas by friends and family who knew her. Most people knew her as Penny. My sisters and I will always remember her for the love she brought to our world, because she was much more than just Penny to us. She was our mother.

Rob Salisbury

Share what you have learnt
with your own children –
it can help them in countless ways.

HELP YOURSELF

Funny thing, advice. Most people only ask for it when they don't want to accept the truth they already know. Others offer it freely because they're not using it. Still, it can have hidden benefits. I never cease to be amazed at the number of times I have helped others and found I was helping myself – a process in which the benefit is returned many times over.

In my seminars I put forward philosophies such as 'Don't spread the negatives, share the positives', and, by constant repetition, I find myself taking my own advice and improving the quality of my life.

This thought came to mind recently when I was exhorting my clients to try to remember any statements, actions or attitudes that may have had a negative influence on their ability to access their sense of humour and joy in living. They were then asked to share it with someone and expunge it from their subconscious – a cheap form of psychoanalysis!

Teaching this caused me to reflect on my wartime child-hood in England (some of you may remember the War – it was in all the papers!). Living in a potential invasion area I was supposed to be evacuated into the care of a country family but my dear grandmother ('Nan' as I called her) wouldn't hear of it so she took me and my elder brother to Devon for the duration.

This resulted in me having the great good fortune to spend my formative years with the most remarkable human being I have ever known. Nan unconsciously instilled in me the natural ability to access joy in adversity as well as to give thanks for the gift of life by enjoying (nearly) every moment of it.

Occasional bombing raids were noisy and frightening occasions and Nan constantly called on her considerable powers of humour and imagination to reassure me of the safety and security that she represented.

I remember quite clearly, when I was about six years old, passing a bomb site. Among the rubble some rough grass was growing with some yellow dandelions – small patches of green and yellow among the blackened and dusty remains. My grandmother paused and said, 'Do you see that? What has happened here is an ugly German has destroyed an ugly building put there by an ugly Englishman. But God is making it pretty again. All the noise and destruction in the world won't ever defeat God. He'll always make it pretty again – no matter what we do.'

How many could find such beauty amidst the horror of war? That amazing perspective; that fantastic way of looking at life; that ability to turn an apparent negative into a powerful positive has stayed with me all my life. By observing Nan and her attitudes to life and people, I learnt to try to make each environment I step into a more pleasant place to be, and, in this way, help others and help myself.

Johnny Pace

*You can turn a negative into a positive by
changing the way you look at life.*

TRIUMPH FROM TRAGEDY

I used to be a victim. A victim of life and its circumstances. Then one day I discovered that all my tragedies brought gifts to me. I discovered that life's tragedies were just my turning points – turning points to a brighter future.

My awakening to this gift came at the time of my dad's death. A tragedy in every sense, my dad died at fifty years of age from a brain tumour. He was an affable, fun-loving man who attracted people everywhere. When he collapsed, walking in the street one day, it was a complete shock to everyone.

I was living in America at the time and jumped on a plane as soon as I heard. I was shocked when I saw Dad that first time, propped up in the hospital bed. Fortunately, I had no commitments back in America so I devoted my time to my father. I would go to the hospital at six o'clock every morning and stay with him until around lunch time, when my stepmother Kerry would come in and spend the afternoon with him. I learnt more about my dad over the next few months than I ever imagined I could in a lifetime.

He was critically ill, so for the first time in his life he allowed me to help him. It was a humiliating experience for a totally independent man to be looked after, but I worked with him to change his perspective so he could understand that it didn't reflect poorly on him.

As we talked, Dad learnt a few things about me too. We talked about everything. I introduced him to alternative thinking on disease and the possibility that he could cure himself. I read books to him. I was there for him in many of the ways I would have liked him to have been there for me when I was a little boy. Funny how life turns around. Here I was, like a father.

Then it ended as quickly as it started. One morning Dad asked me to close the curtains. He called me close. He told me that my stepmother had given him an ultimatum: 'Either stop seeing your sons or I will leave you.' Dad defended Kerry's position. I was flabbergasted, then an amazing clarity descended upon me. I realised that Dad was making the only choice he felt was available to him. So I stopped resisting. I thanked him for sharing with me the reason for his decision. I told him that I loved him and would always be there if he needed me. I remembered how, when I was a boy, the one thing I wanted from him was the space 'to make my own bed and lie in it'. He'd never given me that space, but it was important for me to be able to give it to him.

I told him it would only take a message and I would be back. Then I left. Lots of people judged Kerry for giving Dad that ultimatum, and many also judged Dad for not resisting. I chose to turn the corner and flow with life, believing that I would still have the opportunity to say goodbye.

About eight months later I received a message from a family friend that Dad wanted to see my brothers and me. We arrived at his home and Kerry wouldn't let us in. It caused my brothers lots of pain. For me it was another turning point. Soon after, Dad was put into palliative care for his final days. The nurses were told we were not to be allowed to visit.

One day I received a call telling me Kerry's visiting schedule. I realised again that the world is full of good people. It was a nurse of great charity, sympathetic to our situation, telling me when she would be on duty. My brothers and I visited the same day. Looking at Dad was heartbreaking. He had wasted away to a shadow of the strong and determined man I knew. I went to him and held his hand. I told him I loved him, that I had always respected his choices and that my heart would always be open to him. Then I said goodbye. My youngest brother, Graeme, was with me. He said his own goodbyes and then we left.

I had a strong sense that Dad had been waiting for us. That night he died.

I had expected to be overcome with grief, but I wasn't. I felt joyous that he was finally freed from all the challenges of mortal life, no longer a victim, no longer in pain. At first I judged myself for feeling this way. I felt unworthy and that I was bad. But only for a moment. Then I realised that I had faced yet another turning point – I could choose whether to celebrate a passing or wallow in grief.

That night I had a vivid sense of my father coming to reside in my heart. Now I feel like he is with me everywhere. Free of his human body he is loving and kind. Finally, after years of striving to achieve, to impress and to earn his love, my dad has given me the gift of unconditional love.

From every tragedy we can build a triumph. It simply takes
the realisation that a tragedy is a turning point showing you the
way to grow – a bend in the path of your private journey. A true
gift from God.

Rod Douglas

Recognise, and accept, that some situations
are beyond your control then
rise above your disappointments.

It's Nice to
Know You Can

I hated Thursday afternoons. To a pimply, awkward, foreign-born teenager, dancing class was agony. Lined up in our baggy uniforms and rubber-soled school shoes against one wall of the assembly hall, facing the mob from the boys' school up the road, we watched in wonder and disbelief as our instructors, the svelte black-haired beauty and her tall prince charming, glided faultlessly between us.

Trying to survive the stampede of boys galloping across the hall to choose a partner was almost as hard as trying to reproduce the graceful and effortless steps of our instructors. Why did all the dags with two left feet fight over the right to drag me around the floor, tripping over their own feet as well as mine? Conversation was never easy when counting your steps – one-two-three, one-two-three – and nonexistent after spelling your surname to a Bill Smith every time we changed partners.

Then, a few weeks into second term, we got new teachers.

Strictly Ballroom they were not. The amazon and her dwarf brought real life into dancing class.

He clasped her firmly around the waist, his nose between her large and bouncy breasts. 'Slow, slow, quick-quick, slow!' she commanded above his head, trying to teach us the foxtrot. We tried, we really tried, but failure was a fact of life. They watched us for a while and came up with a solution.

'Take off your shoes,' the amazon roared.

We did. It was a revelation. Freed of the rubber soles which glued us to the floor, we started to make progress. Nobody cared about smelly feet – we were dancing! By the end of term things were looking up. By year's end we were waltzing, foxtrotting and tangoing well enough to say that we could dance. The stress receded, the pimples went and the boys no longer asked, 'Rita who?'

Many years later it is a Saturday night and I am bopping around to a Sri Lankan Afro-Cuban band, my feet in samba mode, and I'm feeling really pleased with myself. You don't really need to know how to dance these days, but it's nice to know you can.

Rita Avdiev

When faced with a problem, free your mind
and think creatively –
the possibilities will be endless.

The Value of Experience

When we lived in Auckland, the glass-panelled front door of our house could be locked in two ways. The lock we always used could only be operated by a key. The other lock, which we didn't use, was operated by a button on the door handle inside and a key which once went into the handle on the outside. This key had been lost by the former owners and we had never bothered to get a new one cut as the other lock sufficed to secure the door. We were always careful not to push the button in on the door handle before we left the house, so we never had a problem. Then one day we forgot to tell a house guest about the extra door handle.

Our guest had decided to leave the house while we were out on an errand so she 'helpfully' secured all the windows and pushed the button in on the front door handle before departing. We returned to find ourselves unable to get in! After trying to open several windows without success, I realised with a sinking feeling that I would have to force an entry into the house.

I'd no sooner smashed the small glass panel in the front door and released the button to let ourselves in when my wife pointed out, to my chagrin, that I had broken some expensive textured glass when I could have achieved the same result by breaking a panel of plain glass in a nearby French window. I thanked her for this observation but reminded her with as much dignity as I could that what was done was done and that there was no point in discussing it any further.

The evening after the glazier had been to replace the panel in the front door, a friend called to pick us up for a book-club meeting and he drew my attention to a tiny piece of broken glass by the front door. I explained how I'd had to break the glass in the door to release the locking button and then showed him how the button was pushed in. The only problem was, I forgot to release the button again so, a few minutes later, when we all left the house, both locks were engaged instead of the usual one. This frustrating fact became all too clear when we arrived home and tried to get in. Again, I found all the windows secured and once again I was faced with the annoying prospect of having to break some glass in order to get in.

This is where my all too recent experience proved to be of value. I remembered what my wife had pointed out to me two days before and, not wanting to make the same mistake again, I broke the less expensive clear glass panel in the French window. And that is the reason why, despite all the experience mankind has had though the ages, the world is still in the mess it's in today.

Peter Sumner

After you make a mistake, step back,
think it through and learn your lesson.

THE ROOSTER
NEXT DOOR

I live on a 650-acre farm in the foothills of the Snowy Mountains in Victoria. It's tranquil, it's beautiful and my wife Carla and I have chosen to make it our home. We are part of a team of people who run a beautiful health retreat, teaching meditation and yoga and providing organically grown vegetarian meals. Our work here gives us the opportunity to serve others.

We meet many people from Melbourne who are caught up in the rat race and come here to unwind. One of the visitors has become a good friend. He's a focused businessman with clearly defined goals. When he started his business ten years ago, one of his goals was to move into a mansion before the age of forty.

He has achieved an awful lot of goals along the way, but none that he was more excited about than this one. We saw him the day he purchased the property at auction. He was, as the expression goes, over the moon. It was exactly what he'd visualised ten years before. He had a list of thirty things he was looking for and this house had twenty-eight of them. In the four months between purchase and settlement, we heard plenty about the home. We were given brochures, a room-by-room description and an elaborate explanation of how the home would be used.

About three weeks after he and his family moved in, we made the pilgrimage to see this new home. We were greeted at the door with gestures of grandeur and given a forty-five minute tour of all of the wonderful aspects of the home. The thing I enjoyed the most was the beautiful botanical garden surrounding the home. The waterfall flowing into the crystal-clear pool lined with tropical green tiles was also very special. After our tour we sat down for a cup of tea and my friend began to tell us his problems. He said he couldn't believe it: the first night in the home he was woken at quarter past three in the morning by a rooster.

'Here we are in a densely populated suburb of Melbourne and my neighbours have a rooster!' Well, he was on a mission to eliminate that rooster. He spoke to all his neighbours (except the one with the rooster) to find out if it was a concern to anyone else. As his was the only home with two storeys, and his bedroom was on the corner facing the rooster's perch, none of the other neighbours even heard the rooster.

All he could do was talk about how frustrated he was with the rooster. It consumed him so much he wasn't able to enjoy the home. It made me think that all of us have roosters in our lives and often they are trying to wake us up to something – in this case to switch focus from mansions and material things to an appreciation of the people and special moments in our lives. Yet we get so caught up in getting rid of the roosters that we miss the lessons behind them.

The next time I spoke to my friend he told me how, after

a long, drawn-out campaign, the rooster was now gone. I mentioned I would be coming to Melbourne and he said he would try and squeeze me into his hectic schedule for a hit of tennis one evening under the lights in his back yard. He told me about his latest projects and how he was far too busy to come up with the kids and visit us. I thought to myself, the rooster is gone but the message behind it hasn't hit home yet.

A week later we were playing tennis in his back yard when I went to retrieve a ball along the fence and I noticed a rat running behind the vines. I made a comment and was told that the rooster problem had now been replaced by rodent problem. The chook house next door had been torn down and underneath it was a rats' nest and they were now everywhere. I just shook my head and served.

Six months later I was working in Melbourne as a consultant when my friend walked into my office with a smile from ear to ear. I had known him for more than seven years and I had never seem him look so happy. He explained that he had just decided to simplify his life and I was the first person to know. He told me the mansion was to be sold and the high-paced schedule and weekly travel to become a thing of the past – it was time to be with the family. The rooster's wake-up call had now been acknowledged.

My friend had the courage to go beyond the illusory dream and embrace the people in his life with love, honesty and service. His story will always be an important reminder to me to tune into the lessons life is trying to teach me.

Neal Hoptman

A NOTE FROM DANIEL: I am the good friend Neal talks about in this story. The mansion he is referring to is on North Road in the bayside suburbs of Melbourne. This book never would have been published if I still had my self-centred outlook on life. I hope the messages in this book are of tremendous value to you, as they are to me.

Listen to the annoyances in your life
and the lessons they may be
trying to teach you.

JOY

I stopped mid-sentence in wonder and began reading the poem again:

> Some of you say,
> 'Joy is greater than sorrow,' and others say, 'Nay, sorrow is the greater.'
> But I say unto you, they are inseparable.
> Together they come, and when one sits alone with you at your board,
> remember that the other is asleep upon your bed.

The Lebanese poet/philosopher Kahlil Gibran penned these gentle words early this century. To me they said 'When sadness is with me, happiness sleeps on my pillow'.

Gibran was a lyrical poet who enchanted his audiences first in the Middle East and then the rest of the world. His book of verse, *The Prophet*, had been given to me by a young girl who was leaving to live on a kibbutz in Israel. His words moved me to tears since, at the time, my life was rather sad. I felt trapped in a situation I neither liked nor wanted, and the pain of my existence seemed endless – there was no golden future.

Yet here was someone telling me that happiness *was* in my life and at some time in the future it would have to awaken from its sleep. I would just have to wait; there was a kinder time coming to me. So I moved on with a positive mind.

Many times over the last three decades, when the wheel has been down and sadness has been with me, I have read Kahlil Gibran's book and been uplifted.

Virginia Hellier

*Re-read an inspiring book when
your soul needs nurturing.*

RISING ABOVE
IT ALL

I stepped from the taxi at Brisbane Airport in the late afternoon and noticed that the clouds looked even more ominous than they had when I left the city. The wind had picked up and was literally blowing a gale; rain was imminent.

'They'll probably delay the flight,' I remarked to my travelling companion, who, as a very nervous flier, seemed greatly relieved upon hearing my 'expert opinion'.

We checked in and made our way to the departure lounge. Through the huge windows we could see the ground crew battling their way around the tarmac, loading baggage and making their final checks as the high winds and now heavy rain lashed the area.

Once on board we could actually feel the wind under the wings lifting the large aircraft with considerable force. The thought occurred to me that I had never boarded a plane under such adverse conditions. I looked at my friend and I noticed that his knuckles were white as he gripped the armrest and waited for our exit from the loading gantry.

We slowly made our way to the end of the runway, the wind and rain buffeting the aircraft with increasing fury. After a slight delay (which I imagined to be a final plea from the control tower not to 'risk it'!) we began to thunder down the long runway, the engines on the big 767 appearing to strain somewhat as they tried to lift this huge plane into the wild bleak yonder.

Once airborne the turbulence became very pronounced, with the plane being thrown around in a way you'd expect with a much smaller aircraft. It continued for what seemed to be an eternity (in reality about three minutes) and I was beginning to wonder how my friend (and I for that matter) would cope if this was going to last all the way to Sydney.

And then it happened. In an instant we broke through the heavy clouds into brilliant sunshine. There was an audible sigh from the passengers as the bumps and thumps gave way to a velvety smooth ride. The experts in the cockpit and, presumably on the ground, had known something my companion hadn't: the storm was very localised. There was sunshine above and clear blue skies.

During the flight, as I reflected on our experiences, I couldn't help but think, 'Hey, every day can be sunny if we can only get enough altitude!'

Graham Agnew

Don't worry unnecessarily;
nothing is as terrifying
as it first appears.

A Wondrous
Experience

Nothing could have prepared me for this event or its aftermath. No one really managed to convey the full impact of how a few hours could irrevocably change your life. Since that time I have often reflected on how ill-prepared I was for the tumultuous change – indeed, how ill-prepared I have been at each subsequent cycle. Somehow circumstances seem to change and one adapts; somehow we all seem to survive and move into the next phase.

In those preparatory months the process seemed interminable: nausea, tiredness, exhaustion and difficulty in concentrating. I quickly established a reputation for being able to fall asleep anywhere. In fact, I am regarded by many of my friends as the only person they have ever known to fall asleep at every single dinner party they have each attended. Then there was my decreasing mobility and increasing vagueness; the latter giving me the capacity to leave my wallet or handbag in public places. I see myself dozing in a chair in the early afternoon; balancing food on my huge built-in dinner tray; somehow staggering on with my normal workload.

Suddenly anxiety and fear: something is happening, but it is a month too early; this couldn't possibly be the real thing. Severe back pain competes with other, strange sensations, but I am still disbelieving. This couldn't be contractions, could it? Not a month early! I don't even have the case packed. Many hours later there is a frantic rush to the hospital. Reality dawns that this is the real thing – the contractions are only five minutes apart. After much pain, discomfort, huffing and puffing, my daughter is born.

Joy . . . wonderment . . . pride, and a surge of protectiveness. Nothing prepared me for the range of emotions; especially the joy. Nothing before or since has come close to the exquisite pleasure of holding this tiny human being in my arms for the first time – how had I managed to create such a perfect being? Indescribable joy!

Since that time there have been many sleepless nights, temper tantrums, great moments of pleasure, giggles, laughter, fear and worry. And much guilt about returning to work.

Now, thirteen years later, I listen to those with older children who say that the girls become reasonable again at about the age of eighteen. So I have only five years to go – not a life sentence! Even now there are moments of real closeness (in-between the times when strangulation seems a good option!). Also, increasingly, there are meetings of the mind as well as the heart and it is possible to look forward to the next thirteen years with real enthusiasm.

If many of the greatest moments of our lives are in some

way bound up with sharing wondrous experiences with our children, then the greatest of them all must still be the moment of pure joy when we first see our newborn child.

Merran Kelsall

Relive joyous moments to carry you
through trying times.

THE VENDOR
IN NAIROBI

Years ago, while travelling overland through Africa, I was camped outside Nairobi for a few weeks. Each day I visited the local open market and always purchased our rice and other staple foods from the same vendor because he 'over delivered'.

The vendor's strategy was simple: when he was measuring rice with his hand-held balance, the weights were put on one side, the rice was put on the other. As the amount of rice approached the correct weight, he would slow down and add an extra handful of rice, which tipped the scale in my favour.

The other vendors took a different strategy. They placed too much rice onto the scale and then slowly removed rice until the balance was reached. Big difference – the vendor I used added on, the others took away. In the end, the weight I received was the

same but somehow I felt better about buying from the vendor who
'over delivered'.

Daniel Johnson

*Be known as a person who gives
rather than takes.*

THE WORLD IN
YOUR OWN
BACK YARD

Have you ever had times when you were so broke you couldn't afford a summer holiday? We had this happen a few years back and we decided that we wouldn't sit around feeling poor; we'd gather up the few bucks we did have and give ourselves a world trip. Of course, it helped that we lived in Melbourne, which must have the most cosmopolitan range of restaurants in the world.

Our voyage commenced in a favourite city of mine, Istanbul. We got there via a restaurant in Brunswick Street, Fitzroy; it didn't quite have the view you get from a cafe under the Galata Bridge, but the food was as good, the music was authentic, and the owner even asked us which country we'd come from, our tourist disguise was so good.

Next day at Victoria Street, Richmond, we discovered Ho Chi Minh City, eating in a cafe that came straight out of the Orient, with huge seafood and noodle soups at $5 a bowl.

In the same spirit of adventure we visited the south of France, enjoying food and a seascape that would can Cannes, at a restaurant on the St Kilda foreshore. And what better way to conclude a summer's lunch than by visiting Vienna for cakes, by way of the numerous patisseries in Acland Street, St Kilda?

As this game progressed, the magic was everywhere. We even spent a few days at a lovely old guesthouse in Queenscliff, with all the old-world charm of a seaside hotel in the south of England.

Then we drove along the cliff road through pretty Cornish fishing villages, though on this side of the world we were travelling along the Great Ocean Road and the villages we visited were Lorne and Apollo Bay, not St Ives and St Just.

Italy and Spain were not far away. We experienced all the bustle and atmosphere of Florence at the Victoria Market on a Sunday and in the evening we watched flamenco dancers at a tapas bar in Johnson Street, Fitzroy.

Before our holiday was over we had visited Greece, Lebanon, Thailand, India and China. Half the pleasure of an overseas trip is walking through foreign streets and enjoying the exotic foods. So, when you can't afford the real thing, dig out your sunglasses and sense of wonder and create your own world trip.

Ray Beatty

Make the best and most of what you have.

Big V

In the autumn in North America geese head south for the winter flying along in a 'V' formation. You might be interested to know what researchers have discovered about why they fly that way, and what we can learn from this.

- It has been realised that as each bird flaps its wings, it creates an uplift for the bird immediately following. By flying in a 'V' formation, the whole flock adds at least 71 per cent to its flying range than if each bird flew alone. *People who share a common direction and sense of community can get where they are going quicker and easier because they are travelling on the thrust of each other.*

- Whenever a goose falls out of formation, it suddenly feels the drag and resistance of trying to go it alone, and quickly gets back into formation to take advantage of the lifting power of the bird immediately in front.

People who 'stay in formation' with others who are headed in the same direction will get there quickly with energy to spare.

- When the lead goose gets tired, it rotates back in the wing and another goose flies 'point'.
  It pays to take turns doing hard jobs.

- The geese honk from behind to encourage those up front to keep up their speed.
  Do we always give positive messages when we honk from behind?

- Finally, when a goose gets sick or is wounded by gunshot and falls out, two geese fall out of formation and follow it down to help and protect it. They stay with it until it is either able to fly or until it is dead and then they launch out on their own with another formation to catch up to their own group again.
  If we have the sense of a goose we will stand by each other like that.

Author unknown
Submitted by Barbara Pettigrew

*Life's much easier when you work
together with others to achieve
a common goal.*

A PEARL
OF WISDOM

This expression was given to me by a very dear friend who always used to use it and which I also use in sharing with my colleagues the need to push things forward: 'gentle pressure relentlessly applied'.

Brian Harries

*Success will come to those who are
the most persistent.*

HIGHS AND LOWS

Coming from a warm, friendly and comfortable background, I was not in any way prepared for the depth of life's lows or, indeed, for the joys of its highs.

At sixteen years of age, a young innocent and a sports fanatic, I met my future husband – a sophisticated man who worked, had a car and a house. Studies were then abandoned and I begged and pleaded to leave school. My poor, pressured parents agreed and I went to work with my father in his pharmacy.

My first glimpse of business was a rude awakening. On my first day, a customer asked for a packet of 'Durex'; red-faced, I eventually worked out what he required. Later I told my father that the window display was disgusting, so he suggested I dismantle and redo it. I immediately dismantled it but then realised I had no idea how to put it back – of course, the professional window dresser had to be recalled to rectify the effects of my over-zealous enthusiasm.

These events seemed to set a pattern in my life, and I dived into full-time motherhood in the same way I had leapt into my first day at work. However, when full-time parenting did not give me the stimulation I needed, I decided to return to the workforce. The response from friends was shock, horror! How could I leave my children? They might become delinquents or drug addicts. But I was not deterred. I adore my family and have always made time to be with them and to develop my relationships with my daughter and son. Business life was not easy, especially when people I thought I could trust let me down, but the rewards were many.

Many years later I had a successful business, I had remarried to a wonderful, supportive man and my two fantastic children were making headway in their own lives. In fact, my son had joined me in the business, so we developed a strong professional relationship as a bonus. This business was sold after nineteen years and both my son and I moved on to the next business project. This was later sold during the depth of the recession at a huge loss. At the time I thought the end of the world had arrived, but I picked up, went into business again and moved forward.

I have found that working is my way of surviving a crisis. In hindsight, the break-up of a marriage, the normal concerns in business, and raising my two children for several years on my own were trying times but these lows all faded into insignificance when I was told that my son had suicided on 21 March 1993. My world crashed. I was overcome with grief and so many questions: Why him? Why now? Why me? To survive, I built a shield around me and felt no joy in living. Then, slowly, I turned to work again to occupy my mind. I found by working long hours that I gradually returned to some normality. But just as important, perhaps more important, was the support and encouragement of both my daughter and husband.

Today I have the same zealousness for life and high energy I've always had, but there is a part of me that is still grieving. Though I cannot share with my son, in the flesh, the joys of living, in quiet times I do tell him what has been happening in my life. He may not be here in body, but I am sure his spirit is with us.

Brenda Rossmann

*During hard times, balance the need
to 'keep busy' with the support
of family and friends.*

An Honest
Day's Work

My first job after leaving school was working in the insurance industry. I had been working for six months when I was invited to the
'Insurance Ball', which was being held on a Wednesday night. Like
all young Australians, I could not resist the chance to get dressed up
in a dinner suit and take a lovely girl to a special occasion. Our group
had a great time and partied on until the early hours of the morning.

The next day I rang my supervisor and told him I was feeling too unwell to come into work, when in fact I was just too tired.
I slept until lunch time and then relaxed around the house.

My father, who always left for work at 6 a.m., was surprised to find me at home when he returned from work that
evening. He inquired why and I told him about my late night and
how I was too tired to go to work. After listening to my excuse he
asked me if it were my business would I have done the same thing?
He also told me how disappointed he was in me and proceeded to

talk about honesty and winners. He then asked me to report to my supervisor the next day and tell him the real reason I didn't attend work the day before. He said I was to ask if I could make up for the day I missed by working on Saturday.

The next morning, after a fairly sleepless night, I got up very early, dressed and went off to work by tram. It was dark and unpleasant weather. I arrived too early and the office was locked, so I had to walk around the city, frozen and depressed.

When I got back to the office, one of the managers was there. He was surprised to see me there so early, but I couldn't tell him why. As soon as my supervisor came in I went to his office and told him of my weak effort the day before and asked if could I make the time up by working the next Saturday. He smiled at me and said that it would be excellent and that he would also advise the general manager of my decision. He said the manager had also been at the Insurance Ball and had noted one or two of his staff were really enjoying themselves. I had not even been aware that the general manager had been at the ball until then.

Saturday was always my favourite sports day and working all day certainly gave me an insight into my father's way of life. I felt better when I had done the work which was left for me to complete on that day. The general manager also came in to work for a couple of hours and I got to speak to him for a while, which made the day a little better.

My father, who retired after thirty-four years as an engineer with an aircraft manufacturer, had only taken five days sick leave in all those years. In the last month of his employment, however, he was burnt on the arms during an accident and had to take some leave – yet he still managed to go to work for part of that time as he didn't want to let the team down.

I received a job advancement opportunity with the company much earlier than expected and I put a lot of this down to the fact that I'd learnt a valuable lesson at an early age. I had learnt to try very hard to do an honest day's work for an honest day's pay.

It is interesting to note that my father has continued to uphold these same values throughout his life. At the age of eighty-three he went to the Victorian Racing Club to apply for a job during the Spring Racing Carnival to be one of those guys in the white coats who direct you or who ensure you have paid to get into the races. The interviewer asked, 'I suppose you are pushing eighty, Frank,' to which my father replied, 'Yes.' Dad told me about this later and I jibed him about his honesty. He said the interviewer had not asked him which *way* he was pushing eighty, and that, at his age, he was pushing it *down*! Dad got the job, loved every minute of it, and would have loved to do it again the following year, but the rules had changed.

At eighty-eight years of age my father still lives by the rules and I hope that the 'apple has not fallen too far from the tree'.

Neil Tresidder

*Hard work and honesty generate inner peace
and a sense of accomplishment.*

BEST AND
FAIREST

'There's no doubt about it, you're a real champion!' my school-teacher and coach would say with conviction. These words reinforced my belief that I was doing something extra special as captain of the under-nine Seaford State School Australian Rules football team.

In spite of my size, I knew my strengths. When I got hold of the ball, no one could catch me. Like the wind, I'd run that ball to the goal square in a flash from anywhere on the field. The problem was, I was the world's worst kick and had no way of knowing where the ball might end up once it left my boot. I countered this tendency to 'spray' the ball by striving to kick my goals a foot *away* from the goal posts – or setting someone else up to kick them for me.

No one seemed to notice this serious shortcoming because I kept getting the scores on the board. In their eyes I was a real champion. I fervently shared their belief.

But with David Stelling on the soccer field, it was a different story. He was resigned to the fact that he was a rotten kick and
he knew that everyone else felt the same way about him too. No
matter how hard he tried, the ball just never seemed to go where
he wanted it to.

David recalls the day he was sitting on the bench as twelfth
man in the inter-club semi-finals with little chance of playing in the
match. At the end of a nail-biting second half, both teams were tied
with two points each. This called for a penalty shoot-out of an
alternate five kicks each team. The pressure was such that despite
superhuman efforts from both sides, no one could break through.

As a winner must be established in a finals match, the five-
kick penalty shoot-out had to be repeated. What's more, the same
player can't have two goes in the one sequence so, as David put it,
'They were forced to turn to the dregs.'

It was with a pounding heart that he walked on to the
pitch as the team's last-ditch effort. All eyes were on him as he nervously jogged in to kick the ball. The thought ran through his
head, 'You watch me botch this.' He didn't let himself down. His
toe dug deep into the turf just as he connected with the ball.

Expecting an explosive attempt to breach his defence, the
goalie was already spread-eagled to block it. But the ball had other
ideas. It lazily skewered sideways and, to the utter amazement of
everybody, dribbled past the desperate clutches of the defender
and into the net.

The crowd went absolutely berserk and David was chaired
off the field as a match-winning hero, his wobbly kicks of the past
instantly forgotten. In their eyes, this penalty shot was one for the
history books. A master stroke of sheer genius – and they never let
him forget it.

David Stelling now had a fine reputation to live up to. He was a champion kick and a semi-finals winner! The following year, not only did he captain the team to success, he also won the club's Best and Fairest award.

David learnt two things from this experience: you don't have to be the best to be a winner; and you most certainly are what you believe you are.

Laurie Smale

Believe you can succeed and you will.

TAKING ACTION

LEARNING FROM LIFE

Use this Action Planner to turn the messages in this

chapter into reality in your life. Turn to pages xvi–xvii to

learn the six simple steps you need to know to make the

most of this Action Planner and to enhance your life.

ACTION STEP

If you are challenged by some tragedy or adversity
in your life, join a support group – there is so much
to learn from others facing a similar challenge.

MY SPECIFIC ACTION STEP

....

....

....

....

....

....

ACTION STEP

Write a story about an important lesson
you have learnt. Writing it down
will put it into perspective.

MY SPECIFIC ACTION STEP

....

....

....

....

....

....

ACTION STEP

After overcoming a major problem or annoyance in your life, sit down and write out the problem, the solution and what you learnt. Review it the next time you are facing a similar problem.

MY SPECIFIC ACTION STEP

....

....

....

....

....

....

ACTION STEP

Ask a friend for the name of a book or a film that has made a major impact on their life; read the book or watch the movie then discuss what you learnt with your friend.

MY SPECIFIC ACTION STEP

....

....

....

....

....

....

ACTION STEP

Have a heart to heart with a friend this week.
Recall a meaningful experience you both shared,
and talk about what you learnt.

MY SPECIFIC ACTION STEP

....

....

....

....

....

....

ACTION STEP

Go to your local library and select an
autobiography written by someone you admire.
Read it all.

MY SPECIFIC ACTION STEP

....

....

....

....

....

....

BIOGRAPHIES

PRUE ACTON, as one of Australia's leading fashion designers, is a legend in her own time. In the sixties, at age nineteen, she opened a business as a young designer, achieved fame and success and was heralded as the 'Mary Quant' of Australian fashion.

Three years ago she closed the manufacturing and retailing side of her business to concentrate on design and teaching fashion. She also returned to life drawing to renew her painting skills with Clifton Pugh. This led her to study with Merv Moriarty, a leading art educator and exhibiting artist.

Prue now lives in southern New South Wales, often returning to Victoria where her family lives. Her ambition is to paint full time and she is currently working towards her next exhibition.

GRAHAM AGNEW has been involved in professional speaking in one form or another for almost two decades. With a successful background in the fields of marketing and public relations, Graham is well qualified to address most issues relating to personal and professional development. For a number of years he worked in the Marketing Division of BP Australia Ltd and today he is an Instructor with the internationally acclaimed Dale Carnegie organisation and a very popular Convention Speaker.

Graham's full-time occupation is that of Senior Minister of the Marion Church of Christ, one of the largest Protestant churches in Adelaide, South Australia, with a multiple staff, an extensive community welfare program and Sunday attendances of just under 600!

BASIL ATKINSON began his working life fifty years ago as a writer. He then moved on to work with tourism bodies, developmental programs in the Bahamas and the South Pacific, and as an industry leader in his home state of Western Australia. He has spent the last five years in Melbourne and has returned to writing, trying his hand at novels.

In 1994 he was made a member of the Order of Australia for his services to international tourism. He is a life member of the Tourism Council of Australia and a long-time Board Member of the Sir Robert Menzies Memorial Foundation.

RITA AVDIEV is the Managing Director of The Avdiev Group, Human Resources and Management Consultants to the property, investment and construction industries, founded in 1981. Educated as an architect, Rita has also worked as an academic, a project manager, and in a quasi-judicial role as a member of the Administrative Appeals Tribunal of Victoria (Planning Division).

Rita is a regular press columnist and a member of many industry and business organisations. With her wide range of professional interests, she often takes an independent and controversial stand on professional, business and industry issues. She is deeply concerned about the future of our society, its patterns of work, education, leisure and lifestyle.

STEVE BARKER is often called 'the invisible man'. His voice is heard around Australia daily, through TV, radio, cinema, telephone and computer messages. Steve also shares his vocal expertise at corporate seminars and business breakfasts. 'Having the "gift of the gab" is one thing, knowing how to present it is quite another!'

Steve has three cats, two daughters and one 'adorable' wife. The

Barker family recently moved from the hectic Sydney pace to the tranquil and clean Blue Mountains. 'We came up for air,' Steve said, 'and at night you can even hear the stars.'

RAY BEATTY started his working life as a journalist. By 1970, after three years of travelling and working in Asia, he found himself working in advertising in Melbourne, where he eventually started his own agency, Ray Beatty Advertising. He also lectures to RMIT University advertising students and writes in *The Bulletin*, Australia's leading news magazine.

BRIAN BEIRNE is a third-generation retailer who holds a Bachelor of Commerce with majors in Accountancy and Economics. His notable appointments in retail include Director of Buying for David Jones in Queensland, Managing Director of McDonnell and East, and Managing Director of the Gold Coast theme park Dreamworld.

In 1992 he relocated to Melbourne to take up the position of General Manager Merchandise, Daimaru Australia. In May 1995 he was appointed Managing Director of Daimaru Australia, the first non-Japanese executive anywhere in the world to be appointed to that role within the Daimaru department store operation.

WAYNE BERRY is the CEO of TOP GUN Business Academy and has shared the platform with some of the world's most famous speakers, including Earl Nightingale, Dr Denis Waitley, Dr Norman Vincent Peale and Tom Hopkins. He was awarded the prestigious APS status by the National Speakers Association of Australia and is an international speaker, trainer and author, and has developed a range of proven training systems for creating profitable companies, increasing sales, building winning teams and creating personal wealth and lasting success. For further details on courses, books, audio and video cassette programs, phone: 61 3 9521 0500 or visit Wayne Berry on the Internet at http://www.topgunba.com.au

COLIN BOCKMAN, a CPS, has achieved career and personal success through his deep understanding of the need for total communication combined with the acute awareness of what is required to shift people's thinking to accept better ways of living and working. As a professional speaker he delivers over 100 high impact presentations each year, which enhance people's perceptions so that they too might achieve 'their ultimate success'.

He can be contacted by first talking with Dianne on phone: 61 3 9764 5022 and fax: 61 3 9764 5001. Audio programs are also available.

ELIZABETH BOYDELL runs her own marketing consultancy, Boydell and Associates, in Melbourne, which mainly deals with destinational marketing, tourism, conventions and special-event marketing. Her travel industry background, of some twenty years, ranges from hotel management, Convention Manager for Jetset Conventions, and Executive Director of the Canberra Visitor and Convention Bureau. Her two forays out of the tourism and hospitality industry saw her work for the Yooralla Society and the Miss Australia Quest, raising funds for disabled people.

Elizabeth enjoys theatre, music, entertaining and reading. She lists her family and friends among her passions, particularly her nephew and two nieces with whom she has a wonderful relationship.

MIKE BRADY is a successful musician and songwriter, having started his career in the mid-sixties with the band MPD Ltd. His success with the song 'Up There Cazaly' and many major advertising campaigns has made him one of the most sought-after jingle- and song-writers. Now with his latest project 'Brady Sings, Brady Talks', Mike has taken on the challenge of expressing his life experiences through public speaking.

FAYE BROWNE leads the thriving Motto Clothing Corporation, an Australian manufacturing/retail business with fourteen stores in Victoria. From the platform of a successful business, Faye is influencing positive change and growth in women through the provision of appropriate information. Currently personally publishing *Motto & You*, a twelve-page quarterly magazine distributed to 15 000 women, she is highly regarded by her peers and is regularly invited to speak at business functions, women's groups and fashion seminars.

Considered a motivational speaker, Faye inspires the desire to achieve in all who listen. Faye, CEO, fashion designer, wife, mother of three, speaker and author, can be contacted on phone: 61 3 9428 9211 or at: 161 Burnely Street, Richmond, Victoria, 3121.

TERRI CALLER emigrated to Australia with her family when she was three years old. At age sixteen she left school to commence an apprenticeship in hairdressing. On completion of the apprenticeship, she travelled with her sister to Europe for one year, experiencing many challenges. When they returned, she opened the first of four salons, which became a very well known and successful venture.

Being a single parent she is proud to say that her seventeen-year-old son is her best friend and the greatest achievement in her life. 'Through him I have found unconditional love,' she says.

OSCAR CARLSON is fifty-five years old and married to Liz. He has two children: Brett, aged twenty-seven, who has brain damage, and Amy, who is in Year Seven at Melbourne Girls' Grammar.

A teacher since 1962, Oscar has taught everything from Matriculation to Prep in New South Wales, South Australia and Victoria. With an impressive background in sporting achievement, he began triathlons at the age of forty-five, competing in over 150 races and being ranked either number one, or in the top three in Australia since.

Oscar's aims now are to assist his family to maximise their options and assist and encourage them to achieve their life goals. He trains forty-five triathletes of all ages to achieve beyond their expectations, and encourages them to be healthy, positive contributors in the community, at work and in everyday life.

LYNDSEY CATTERMOLE is the Founder and Joint Managing Director of Aspect Computing Pty Ltd. It was founded in 1974 and currently has over 800 staff, with offices in Melbourne, Sydney, Canberra, Adelaide, London, Amsterdam and Chicago.

She holds a Bachelor of Science (Microbiology and Genetics) from the

University of Melbourne, and is currently the Chairman of the Women's and Children's Healthcare Network and holds many board positions.

PHILLIPA CHALLIS, JP, ASM. As principal of her own promotions and public relations consultancy, Phillipa Challis has assisted many individuals and organisations to dramatically improve their business promotion, achieve success through personal and corporate development and significantly increase their profits.

She is an Accredited Member of the National Speakers Association of Australia and has presented in Australia and America. She is acknowledged for her positive outlook and for working with people to develop skills that enhance their personal and business growth. Phillipa particularly enjoys speaking in schools and trying to help people lift their self-esteem.

LYNN CHAMPION is an inspirational speaker and author. She is a past president of the New South Wales chapter of the National Speakers Association of Australia, a recent Australian Executive Woman of the Year, an international corporate image award winner, business image strategist and author of the books, *One Minute Money Makers* and *Messages from the Fridge . . . Rich Inspirations for Life*. Lynn is frequently interviewed by the media and is a judge for the Young Achievement Australia Awards. She can be reached at: PO Box 31, Balmain, NSW 2041. Phone: 61 2 9555 1393.

THE HONOURABLE DON CHIPP, AO, spent twenty-six years in federal politics. He served and acted as a Minister in twelve different portfolios and was leader of the House of Representatives.

In 1977 he resigned from the Liberal Party and founded the Australian Democrats. He resigned from the Senate in 1986 after holding the balance of power in Federal Parliament for six years.

He is now happily married for the second time and has two delightful daughters to add to the four children of his previous marriage.

YVONNE CLIFTON is a loving mother of five children and grandmother of two. She enjoys her family, gardening, sewing and a variety of other activities. She lives in Victoria, Australia.

DENNICE COLLETT is a writer and product manager in a leading business publishing house. She has a Bachelor of Music and a Bachelor of Arts (Honours) from the University of Melbourne and a Master of Arts specialising in museum studies through Monash University.

BRAD COOPER, in the last four years, has built his company from the ground to over $100 million. He is founder, Chief Executive and major shareholder of the FAI Home Security Group, one of the fastest-growing companies in Australia today.

Brad is a Director of the Australian Elizabethan Theatre Trust, and is an Adviser to the Board of the Collingwood Football Club.

With no formal education, Brad left school at the age of thirteen, yet his business sales and marketing strategies have experts Tom Peters and Tony Robbins spreading the Brad Cooper story around the world.

KHANH DO has worked as a professional engineer in the energy industry for the last seven years in Melbourne, Victoria. He led the Gas and Fuel team in the 1995 Australian Financial Review Management Championship Competition, which came fourth overall. He also enjoys hang-gliding. Currently he is looking for an international company aiming to expand into Vietnam. He can be contacted at: 66 Yarra Avenue, Reservoir, Victoria, 3073. Phone: 61 3 9478 5252.

ROD DOUGLAS is Australia's leading personal success coach. Teacher, businessman, adventurer, writer and speaker – Rod's expertise comes from doing it!

Amazingly he was a high-school drop-out and has been self-employed since he was eighteen. Rod earned his first million dollars by the age of twenty-three, retired at twenty-five and travelled the world pursuing practical leading-edge technologies, and ideas on success, wealth and happiness. He is available as a speaker and success coach throughout Australia, New Zealand and South-East Asia. Phone: 1800 808 446.

KEVIN EGAN, for the past four years, has been largely involved in the delivery of training workshops, courses and training programs from twenty-minute workshops to twenty-day training programs and everything in between. The topics he delivers include: Personal Effectiveness, Time Management, Team Building, Telephone Skills, Negotiation Skills, Customer Service, Sales Techniques, Interview Skills, Small Business Marketing, Meeting Procedures, Public Speaking, Training the Trainer Level 1, Career Development and Leadership.

He can be contacted at: Level 1, 12 Smolic Court, Tullamarine, Victoria, 3043. Phone: 61 3 9335 1872. Fax: 61 3 9335 2105.

RENNIE ELLIS is a photographer whose work appears regularly in major Australian magazines and has been widely exhibited in Australia and Asia. It is also included in various collections including the National Gallery of Australia and Bibliothèque Nationale in Paris. He is best known for his documentation of popular culture and the demimonde.

He sees his photographic excursions as a series of encounters with other people's lives. He has sixteen books to his credit.

LORRAINE ELLIOTT, MLA, BA, BEd, has been the State Member for Mooroolbark since October 1992 (Liberal Party). Currently Parliamentary Secretary to the Premier for the Arts, Lorraine is a former secondary school teacher in English, English Literature, History and French. She has three adult children, one son-in-law, one husband, one cat, one dog. Lorraine's interests include literature, film, drama, walking and white-water rafting.

EVELYN FIELD is a psychologist in private practice in Toorak, Victoria. She has a general practice, seeing children, adolescents and adults. In addition to her interest in helping people improve their relating skills and protect themselves from all types of bullying, she helps people deal with stress, trauma, depression and personal and work difficulties.

Evelyn speaks professionally in Australia and overseas and uses her model 'Secrets of Relating' as the central core. She is an Accredited Speaking Member of National Speakers Association of Australia and is currently involved in writing a book on dealing with teasing and bullying.

Evelyn is one of the media spokespersons for the Australian Psychological Society and is on the Board of VOCAL. Her phone/fax is: 61 3 9804 7575.

OLGA FLORENINI works in the field of Career Enhancement/ Counselling and Outplacement Services for Malcolm Press and Associates. She began working-life as a recruitment consultant, eventually running her own consultancy. After the birth of her second child, she decided to make a career transition. This involved juggling postgraduate studies, Career Counselling and work, a process which was simultaneously gruelling and fulfilling, but one that has paid off. Olga now works with clients to facilitate their attainment of career and personal goals.

YVONNE FLYNN (née SCHREURS) is Co-director of International Corporate Event Services, a well-established event management company based in Melbourne, which she and her husband Barry have operated since 1981. She has worked in the fields of personnel, staff training, marketing and public relations and thrives on the challenges involved in running this service-based business.

    As a mother of two very busy teenage daughters, she regards her 'private family times' as the most precious and enjoyable rewards in life.

MALCOLM GRAY is featured in the Channel 7 (Melbourne) Hall of Fame. He shared a Logie for the network's coverage of the Ash Wednesday bushfires.

    He is a professional communicator and an award-winning speaker and author of many articles, books, audio tapes and seminar packs, including the Australian classic *Public Speaking*, published by the Business Library of Australia.

    Malcolm is a renowned MC and speaker at conferences, business networks and conventions. He also provides speakers for growing organisations through his company Prospeak OZ. Daniel Johnson and Malcolm Gray are co-authors of the two-cassette seminar pack 'How to be an MC and win your audience over . . . every time!'

MARCIA GRIFFIN is CEO of Pola Cosmetics Australia and New Zealand Pty Ltd, a company she has built from having a solitary salesperson to a sales team of 4500.

    She is also a motivational speaker and keen world traveller. She is currently working on her first book, which traces her journey from school teaching to being one of the few women in the world heading up a Japanese company. Marcia can be contacted on phone: 61 3 9529 5433 and fax: 61 3 9525 0042.

JOHN HADDAD, AM, is an outstanding figure of the Australian tourism industry. He is Deputy Chairman of Crown Management Pty Ltd, and Deputy Chairman of the Federal Hotels Group. Crown Casino won the right to establish the largest Casino in the world in Melbourne. The temporary casino opened in July 1994. John was the Chairman of the Australian Tourist Commission from 1985 to 1995, and is a foundation member of the Melbourne Tourism authority.

In recognition of his contribution to the tourism industry and to the community, he was appointed a Member of the General Division of the Order of Australia in the Queen's Birthday Honours List in 1988. He was also honoured with an Advance Australia Ambassadorship in 1989.

DR JANET HALL is a success coach who inspires people to have the heart to go for it and the discipline to make it. A professional speaker, psychologist and hypnotherapist, Jan is the author of four books, including *Fight Free Families* and *Confident Kids*, and the unique software program 'GoalMaker', which helps you set and monitor your goal achievement over time to encourage maximum success.

To book speaking engagements or order books, please contact Dr Janet Hall by writing to: 2 Glen Street, Hawthorn, Victoria, 3122. Phone: 61 3 9818 1888 or fax: 61 3 9818 8581. Internet: hall@goalmaker.com

JENNIE HAM WASHINGTON commenced modelling in 1958, with assignments in Australia, London, Paris and Milan. She then joined *In Melbourne Tonight* as a regular with Graham Kennedy.

She later started Jennifer Ham and Associates, a public relations company, specialising in fashion, tourism and entertainment. She was responsible for presenting Roy Orbison in Australia and New Zealand and also brought world-famous Vidal Sassoon and his artistic team to Australia, presenting hair shows and seminars in all major cities.

She was a Life Governor of Prince Henry's Hospital and a board member of the Lost Dogs Home. She co-founded the Fundraising Committee for Multiple Sclerosis and founded the Daffodil Committee for the Queensland Cancer Fund.

SIR RUPERT HAMER was a Premier of Victoria for nine years and is now a speaker, reviewer and president of various community enterprises in the fields of health, conservation and the arts. His twenty-three years as a Member of Parliament and earlier five and a half years in the Australian Army in World War II took him to many parts of the world.

VICTORIA HANSEN is an entrepreneur. She trained at Hawkesbury Agricultural College (now the University of Western Sydney) as a Home Economics teacher, graduating in 1979. Since then she has worked in many industries and has been running her own consultancy in marketing, both personal and corporate, since 1991.

She launched Fioricard (Australia) Pty Ltd in 1995, Australia's first centralised flower ordering, date reminder and Frequent Flower™ service, based on the USA's very successful 1800 Flowers.

She has recently returned to her field of expertise as a home economist and is now a presenter with the TV Shopping Network, seen throughout the cable network, with a cooking and craft show each week.

BRIAN HARRIES is Executive General Manager, Crown Towers, Melbourne, the luxury hotel section of the Crown Entertainment complex. With extensive experience in the hotel industry, he has fulfilled the role of General Manager at a number of international five-star hotels. His most recent position was General Manager at the Shangri-La Hotel in Bangkok, which is consistently voted in the top ten hotels in the world.

MICHAEL HARRISON heads a business advisory group specialising in sales and business strategies for the new millennium.

A visionary business thinker, author and professional speaker, he has built several successful businesses and has served on numerous government and corporate boards.

His profit-building sales and business concepts have been adopted by business owners in the United States, the United Kingdom, Asia, Australia and New Zealand.

He can be contacted at: 21st Century Sales Strategies, Suite 14, 116–120 Melbourne Street, North Adelaide, SA, 5006. Telephone: 61 8 8267 6333. Facsimile: 61 8 8267 6363.

VIRGINIA HELLIER, for the last twenty years, has cooked food, talked about food, written about food, taught how to cook food, designed food, created food concepts, created food outlets, combined food and wine, promoted food and food venues, put together food festivals, and travelled the world looking at food.

MURRAY HINE was born in 1954 in Mordialloc, a Melbourne suburb. One of two children, he and his brother attended Mentone Grammar School. He completed a Bachelor of Arts in 1975 and a Diploma of Education in 1976. After teaching English, he worked for APPM from 1980–88 and has since worked for several companies including Pacific Dunlop. In 1994 he joined ACI as Marketing and Sales Manager, and now runs Continental Pet Pacific.

He has been marred for twenty years to Sally. They have three children, aged fourteen, twelve and nine.

MAX HITCHINS, at the time of writing this piece, was the President of National Speakers Association of Australia. He is the author of *Hands on Hospitality: 365 Marketing Ideas; Max's II Marketing Commandments;* and *Fact, Fiction and Fables of the Melbourne Cup.* He can be contacted on phone: 61 2 9369 4411 and fax: 61 2 9369 4320. Email: max@hitchins.com.au

JACK HONE is a professional speaker and consultant who specialises in developing leaders, building confidence and empathy, creating customer excellence and improving professional selling skills. Based in Melbourne, he can be contacted by phone or fax on: 61 3 9438 3776, or write to: PO Box 521 Eltham, Victoria, 3095.

NEAL HOPTMAN is Program Director of the Ontos Health Retreat outside of Buchan in East Gippsland and author of *Help Yourself to Health*. Neal came to Australia in 1982 after meeting his wife, Carla, in Venice. They have been running health enhancement programs at Ontos, teaching people lifestyle skills to improve their wellbeing. They also have established programs in Melbourne and Sydney and recently established a Complementary Therapy Department at Melbourne's Cedar Court Hospital. They can be contacted at Ontos Health Retreat, Buchan Post Office, Victoria, 3885. Phone: 61 3 5155 0295.

JEFF HOOK is a freelance cartoonist, author, illustrator and public speaker. His work appears regularly in the Sunday *Herald Sun*, *Australasian Post* and *Victorian School News*. A former Tasmanian, he joined the Melbourne *Sun News Pictorial* in 1964. He has worked in collaboration with Melbourne writer Keith Dunstan. Together they rode bicycles across the United States as part of the country's Bicentennial celebrations, recording the event in a book titled *It's All Uphill*. He is a member of the Australian Black and White Club, The Realist Artists Guild of Australia, the Illustrators' Association of Australia and is a former President of the Melbourne Press Club. He can be contacted at: 2 Montana Street, Glen Iris, Victoria, 3146, or by phone/fax: 61 3 9809 1560.

PETER HORNHARDT is a passionate and professional presenter. From 'one to one' consultation through training groups of ten to forty and on to conference presentations, he has developed into a master facilitator.

Since 1990 Peter has published a highly successful book and cassette program called *Plan Your Life – Plan Your Career*. He has also written articles and produced audio cassette programs, including 'Time Management', 'Communication Skills' and 'Leadership Beyond 2000', to name a few.

TREVOR HOUSLEY runs a consultancy specialising in Information Technology and Telecommunications. He is a professional development trainer and public speaker on Telecommunications and High Technology issues. He is also a published author of *Data Communications and Teleprocessing Systems*, which was used in many universities around the world over a ten-year period. Trevor likes to write and sketch and plays an average game of golf. He can be reached at: PO Box 189, Gordon, NSW, 2072. Phone: 61 2 9499 2666.

STEVE HUMPHRIES is a martial arts instructor who incorporates integrated learning, using sophisticated methodologies, such as neuro-linguistic programming and kinesiology. He has also benefited from joining Toastmasters International public speaking. Steve can be contacted at: 10 Whittaker Street, Maidstone, Victoria, 3012.

KATE JOHNSON lives in Brekenridge, Colorado, with her husband, Daniel, and their four children. She is active in several family-oriented volunteer organisations and loves outdoor pursuits.

JENNY KEAT is currently running her own small business in personnel consulting. For the last seven years she has built and developed the business into a profile business servicing the garment manufacturing and retail industries.

She grew up in rural north-east Victoria before coming to the big smoke to pursue a career. Commencing a career with a major service company gave her the entree into staff development and training before moving on to personnel consulting. Jenny believes a country upbringing gave her a great balance and understanding of people. She married her soulmate on beautiful Bedarra Island.

MERRAN KELSALL is a financial consultant and company director with over twenty years' professional experience. A partner at BDO Nelson Parkhill until December 1996, she also led BDO's Business Services Division for five years. Her directorships have included the Transport Accident Commission, RMIT, IOOF of Victoria Friendly Society and the North Eastern Health Care Network.

BARRY KNIGHT is an executive recruitment specialist. He established Knight Consulting Group in 1983 and from 1984–1996 he produced a quarterly newsletter, *Knightview*, which was distributed to the clients and associates throughout New Zealand, Australia, the United Kingdom and the United States. *Knightview* became recognised as one of the better publications in the international recruitment industry. Barry is now General Manager, South Island, Morgan & Banks Ltd, and can be reached at: PO Box 4546, Christchurch, New Zealand. Phone: 64 3 379 9000.

JOHAN KRUITHOF is a speaker, author, educator and consultant on personal and corporate quality. His writing credits include the award-winning *Quality Thinking – Thinking Quality* and the bestselling *The Quality Standards Handbook*. Jo is passionate about people and believes that quality, like charity, begins with the individual. He is fascinated by the confluence of technology and philosophy, which he perceives happening at an increasing pace as we near the end of the millennium. To contact Jo, write to: Quality Insights, PO Box 2053, Mount Waverley, Victoria, 3149. Phone: 61 3 9807 4776. Email: qthink@vicnet.net.au

TRUDY LIGHTFOOT specialises in customer service, counter and reception staff, communication and secretarial development. She has a highly motivated style, building up people's self-esteem and encouraging time at work to be more productive and more enjoyable. She values people and emphasises their importance. Trudy can be contacted at the Concord Centre, 289 Ross River Road, Aitkenvale, Queensland, 4817. Phone: 617 4725 2550. Fax: 617 4725 1831. Email:arlo@ultra.net.au

NANETTE LILLEY grew up on a cattle property in south-east Queensland. After her marriage, she and her husband Angus had two sons and moved to a small village in north-western New South Wales, where they were engaged in wheat farming and transport.

In 1972 the Lilleys moved to Brisbane and Nanette has since become one of the leading real-estate agents in Brisbane and in the top 5 per cent of agents Australia wide.

JOHN LOCKWOOD began his business career as a junior employee of Blackburn & Lockwood Real Estate at the age of twenty-five. The company policy then was that you rose through the ranks by your own endeavours. John became a salesman and then, after winning a competition, a manager. This was followed shortly by returning to sales. (At this stage he was not ready for management.)

Again he rose through the company, becoming a manager, and then a director, until, in 1986, he became Managing Director and Chairman of the Board. John decided to franchise the company and by the end of 1986, the number of offices had grown to twenty-one.

In 1992 John sold his interests in Blackburn & Lockwood and resigned to set up his own training organisation, Integrity Management Corporate Sales Training, better known by the acronym I.M.C.A.S.T.

JOAN LUPSON entered the teaching profession for twelve months after completing her HSC at a convent school. She was then asked to work at the Commonwealth Serum Labs where she remained for the next six years. When the war ended she became an air hostess with Australian National Airlines (ANA) and then settled in an accounts office. There she met the writer of the famous letter, who was to become her husband. Still happily married forty-five years later, she has two children: a son Peter, a lawyer; and a daughter Jan, a sales executive with Qantas.

TED MACKNESS is an accredited speaker, trainer and MC with twenty-two years' experience in the Australian speaking industry. He is a long-term member of National Speakers Australia and Toastmasters International. Ted's expertise is in Effective Communication, Leadership/Directorship Techniques, Productive Meetings and Personal Development Skills. His training company, Priority Skills Training Academy, operates in Sydney, Australia. Phone: 61 2 9523 2586.

DOUG MALOUF is one of Australia's most respected professional speakers and authors. He currently works with over 25 000 people a year worldwide, showing them how to increase their presentation, communication and selling skills. Founder VP of the National Association of Speakers, Australia, whose NSW Chapter named him Speaker of the Year. He has authored six books, five cassette programs, three videos and is considered by his peers as the master of audience participation. You can contact him at: DTS International. Phone: 61 2 9360 5111. Fax: 61 2 9360 5199.

ANNE MASSEY is Manager, Partner Marketing, Asia Pacific, for ITT Sheraton Hotels and Resorts, based in Sydney.

Married with three children, Anne's full-time career began eight years ago with the Southern Pacific Hotel Corporation, as Front Desk Manager at Lassiters Casino, Alice Springs. She has been with ITT Sheraton for seven years, starting at Sheraton Alice Springs as Convention Services Manager, then Sheraton Darwin Hotel as Director of Sales, Sheraton Perth Hotel as Convention Services Manager, transferring two years later to Melbourne as Director of Sales for ITT Sheraton Hotels and Resorts, Pacific. She is currently undertaking a Graduate Diploma course through Bond University.

CAMPBELL McCOMAS. Over the past twenty years, in a unique career, former lawyer Campbell McComas has become Australia's leading professional speechmaker, creating over 1400 original characters for conferences, dinners and special events throughout the nation and overseas. He is also well known as moderator of the very popular *World Series Debating* on ABC TV. In 1996 Campbell was awarded an Honorary Doctorate of Letters by the University of New South Wales for eminent service to the community. He is only the second Australian in his field (after Barry Humphries) to be recognised in this way.

MERVYN MORIARTY is a remarkable artist and art educator. His earliest works dating back to the late 1950s were influenced by his teachers Andrew Sibley and John Molvig. Merv, however, soon developed a distinctive independent style. His works have been widely exhibited throughout eastern Australia and he is represented in the Australian National Gallery, Canberra, the Queensland Art Gallery, the New South Wales Art Gallery, the Brisbane City Gallery and in many private collections.

Merv is best known as the Founder of the Australian Flying Art School (AFAS). In 1971, this bold initiative saw Merv, equipped with pilot's licence, take art education to outback Queensland. Within a few years, with support from Clifton Pugh and the then Prime Minister Gough Whitlam, the AFAS came to serve the needs of hundreds of artists living in rural and remote areas.

LEO ORLAND, CFRE, MFIA, has been a professional fundraiser for over fifteen years, three years with the Yooralla Society of Victoria and twelve years with World Vision Australia. He is Victorian President and National Secretary of the Fundraising Institute of Australia. Leo is the Direct Marketing Manager at World Vision, a role which involves creative direction of fundraising materials, marketing information, research and analysis and production of World Vision's printed materials. He also manages World Vision's emergency relief appeals as well as its direct mail program. He has degrees in media, advertising and theology. He is married with three children.

JOHNNY PACE is an entertainer, actor, writer, producer and entrepreneur with thirty-six years' experience in the arts. An Accredited Speaking Member of the National Speakers Association of Australia, he is an accomplished after-dinner speaker who now concentrates his knowledge and experience into workshops and seminars on comedy, humour and humour perspectives. His main seminar topic 'Feeling Good Is Good Business' is in great demand, particularly with high school teachers who need all the help they can get, and accountants, who need it even more!

GEORGE PAUL was born in Budapest, Hungary, in 1939. He emigrated to Australia with his parents in 1951. Married to Susan, he has three children: John, twenty-five; Richard, fourteen; and Sarah, eleven.

He is currently General Manager Retail of the 435-outlet Darrell Lea Chocolate Shops. Prior positions include Director of Stores, David Jones Department Stores, Managing Director Hardy Bros Jewellers and Managing Director of Waltons Bond and Norman Ross.

His greatest influences were his father Tibor, and Eric Greenhalgh, formerly Director of Trading, The John Lewis Partnership, Managing Director of David Jones and Chairman of Waltons Bond. He cites his greatest achievements as having beaten workaholicism, and managing to lead a balanced life.

COLIN PEARCE, based in Adelaide, has the fortunate knack of reducing complex ideas to very simple notions that anyone can understand. This helps him double his clients' sales through training and TV advertising, and it makes him a hit at conventions.

'My family comes first, though,' he says, 'and it's the most complex organisation I deal with. Being dad to four creative and energetic children is my biggest challenge. I'm glad my own dad set me off on the right path.'

BARBARA PETTIGREW says, 'You can take the girl out of the country but you can't take the country out of the girl,' and she's so pleased. 'That openness and honesty may not have made me a million dollars but I have met incredible people, been to amazing places and have some fantastic stories to tell. Every day I meet someone new and learn something new, and welcome the opportunity to help others do the same.'

MARIA PRENDERGAST is a freelance writer and broadcaster, and arts administrator, and lifelong chronic asthmatic. She has written a number of technical and medical books, was a feature writer for Australia Consolidated Press magazines for ten years and has contributed articles to the *Age*, the *Sun Herald* and the *London Observer*. She compiled and published the *Australian Arts Diary* for eighteen years.

BRENDA ROSSMAN, AM, FAIM, has a long career in small business, commencing her first operation – a personnel recruitment business – in 1968 with a start-up capital of $500. This business grew to become a multi-million-dollar organisation, winning several business awards. After selling her first business in 1987 she acquired another in the information industry, which she developed into a national organisation and sold in 1991.

Brenda commenced her fourth career in 1992 in the healthcare industry. She established Medipower, a professional service which provides staff and a much needed home nursing service for both public and private hospitals. Medipower was acquired by FH Faulding in 1996 and Brenda is contracted for the next five years to develop Medipower in each state.

During Brenda's career she has won several awards, and in 1988 she was honoured with an Order of Australia for her contribution to 'Business and Community', in particular to small business.

LEONARD RYZMAN is a popular Australian motivational speaker and author, whose speciality is helping people believe in themselves and convert negative feelings into positive. His entertaining, dynamic presentations achieve results because of the specific ideas given. He uses inspiration, practical steps and humour to help people be their best. He is the author of several books, including *Make Your Own Rainbow*. Leonard can be contacted by writing to: 1/1017 Glenhuntly Road, Caulfield, Victoria, 3162.

ROB SALISBURY, since 1984, has been a full-time trainer, speaker and consultant to over 860 USA-based companies and 165 Australian companies. In representing Tom Hopkins over ten years, Rob has achieved many top awards, including Most Improved Team Player, President's Club Member and Top Sales Manager in Western United States.

Rob has worked on thousands of projects in the United States as well as in Australia for Tom Hopkins, Jim Rohn, Anthony Robbins, Brian Tracy, George Walther, Dr Bob Bays, Zig Ziglar and Jay Abraham. He has helped coordinate more than 3800 training programs for these speakers. Rob's sales teams have produced in excess of $US 80 million in revenue for these speakers. His focus is on teaching people how to promote, market and sell themselves and their businesses more effectively.

MARGARET SEEDSMAN began her working life as a home economist and teacher. She served as Mayor of the former City of Doncaster and Templestowe (now Manningham) in Victoria in 1980, added recreation planning qualifications and moved to Nashville, Tennessee, USA. There she received an award from the State after managing the Tennessee Recreation and Planning Association. She returned to Australia to take up the position of National Executive Director of the Australian Association of Speech and Hearing where she was awarded the coveted Australian Society of Association Executives Gold Award.

More recently she managed ten associations through Dynamic

Association Consultants, her own association management company. She is currently Executive Director of Home-Based Business Australia and focuses on speaking, writing and consulting as Australia's specialist on home-based business.

SHERRILL SELLMAN is an international seminar leader, trainer, author, lecturer and psychotherapist practising in Melbourne. She particularly delights in assisting people to create miracles in their lives.

GRANT SHANKS is a full-time Christchurch-based writer who calls on a lifetime of many and varied experiences to help him communicate with his audience. A former professional hunter and seaman, he also has experience in the recording industry, and as a creative writer in advertising, marketing and radio. He has won many international awards for his work, including CLIO. Grant's non-fiction credits include *A Long Goodnight*, the story of New Zealand's most famous case of euthanasia, and *We Just Want Our Daughter to Live*, the tale of Kelly Turner and her fight for life. Grant can be contacted for your writing project on: phone: 64 3 3372622 or fax: 64 3 3372638.

VIRGINIA SIMMONS has been working in the Technical and Further Education (TAFE) system for nineteen years. She is currently Director of the Kangan Institute of TAFE, a nationally recognised institute in the north-west of Melbourne.

She is one of a family of five children who grew up in Melbourne.

LAURIE SMALE, an inspirational speaker and author, has helped thousands attain professional success and personal fulfilment through shifts in thinking and effective communication – whether they're speaking with one person or in front of a thousand. Yet success did not come easily. Numerically illiterate for most of his life, it was decades before he realised his true potential – the gift of bringing out the best in other people.

Want to make a real difference? Book Laurie for your next conference, workshop, seminar or one-on-one by phoning: 61 3 9890 3224.

MAHGO SMITH ARMSTRONG was born in 1929 and brought up in Belfast, Northern Ireland. In 1949 she went to London to study nursing, following which she studied art and married an Englishman. They had two daughters and lived in London for seven years, then spent three years in Borneo before coming to Australia in 1960.

Divorced in 1979 and remarried in 1983, she lived at Mount Macedon until the Ash Wednesday bushfires when she and her family moved to Queenscliff. Mahgo has worked as a professional painter since 1965.

IAN SPICER, AM, has recently retired as Chief Executive of the Australian Chamber of Commerce and Industry (ACCI), which he was instrumental in forming in 1993. He was also an Employer Adviser to the International Labour Organisation (ILO).

When the Council for Aboriginal Reconciliation was formed in 1991 by special legislation of the Australian Parliament, he was invited to become a member, an appointment he continues to hold.

Ian Spicer's service to business and the community was recognised by an Order of Australia in 1983.

ELIZA STACEY completed her Bachelor of Speech Pathology degree at La Trobe University, Melbourne, in 1996. She has recently moved away from her family and friends to work in rural Australia.

PETER STOKES' initial career was in the army, where he spent many years in Papua New Guinea, Asia and the United States of America as well as on active service in Vietnam. He has commanded an infantry battalion and spent three years as a Military Attaché. He resigned in 1981 to join a national charity as CEO. Peter runs his own training consultancy, ALTER, and is the author of the book *So Now You're a Leader*. He is a graduate of the Royal Military College Duntroon, the USA Army Infantry School, the Indian Staff College and taught at the Australian Command and Staff College.

JANN STUCKEY has entertained, informed and inspired audiences across Australia in her career as a professional speaker for more than a decade. A pioneer of the Australian image industry in 1984, Jann was Queensland State President for the National Speakers Association for 1993 and 1994. A popular and sought-after presenter with a refreshing style, her areas of expertise are communication and presentation skills, customer service and public speaking techniques. Recently she was appointed coach and manager to Perry Cross, Australia's first professional speaker on life support.

PETER SUMNER lost his sight at nineteen through an accident, and, after working in the field of rehabilitation, founded and led an overseas aid and relief organisation. Peter is a gifted writer and platform speaker who has inspired and motivated thousands of audiences in several countries.

PEARL SUMNER, together with her husband, estbalished an International Aid and Development Organisation, presently serving thousands of handicapped people around the world.

Pearl was instrumental in establishing National Speakers Association in New Zealand. She has produced five vocal albums, and writes and speaks widely. Blind since birth, Pearl inspires people to achieve. Her Personal Development Program 'Get Better, Be Better' gives the *'how to'* . . .

IAN TEAGUE is a retired Army Officer who saw active service in Malaya, Borneo and Vietnam. Before retiring he was also a Victorian Public Service Administrator. He has travelled and worked in several countries, including Antarctica, Singapore, South Africa and South America. Prior to his present appointment he was a staff development officer for several years and also a National Park Ranger. He has made many presentations and written articles and papers on a range of subjects, which include Antarctica, leadership management, self-development, training and retirement planning.

NOËLLE TOLLEY divides her life between writing and business and overseas travel as an Export Sales Director. A former freelance journalist and interviewer for the ABC, she cheerfully roams past and future. She has completed her first epic historical novel of the Murray River, *In Looking Glassland*. Home is among fragrant orange groves at 'Ihabi', Renmark, South Australia.

MARK THOMSON is the Managing Director of IMAGINE IF – CREATIVE SOLU-
TIONS, which is a Special Events, Exhibition and Creative Services Business
based in Melbourne. He has been involved with major Displays and Exhibitions both in Australia and internationally. Through IMAGINE IF, Mark actively
supports environmental and social-issue projects through the use of effective
public awareness exhibitions. He personally enjoys travel, camping, movies,
magic, writing and the creative use of his imagination.

   He can be contacted at: IMAGINE IF – CREATIVE SOLUTIONS, PO Box
54, Lower Plenty, Victoria, 3093. Phone: 61 3 9439 5508.

SHARON THOMSON is an accountant in a small chartered accounting firm
in Melbourne. She is a part-time environmental promoter and fundraiser with
Environment Victoria. She also enjoys a good 'chill' as a vocalist working in
an Acapella group, and folk-art furniture-painting when time permits. She can
be contacted at: Unit 6/178 Main Road, Lower Plenty, Victoria, 3039. Phone:
61 3 9439 5508 (home) or 61 3 9867 7711 (work).

NEIL TRESIDDER, born in Melbourne, has worked in all facets of the General Insurance Industry for over thirty years and loves it. He has a passion for
camping in the desert, which he believes gives him a healthy respect for
nature and people. Neil and his wife Wanda live in Gippsland on five acres of
lovely bushland surrounded by trees over 100 years old.

ELIZABETH TRIMBLE is forty-three, divorced, and has two teenage children.
After spending six years in the fashion industry she changed direction to assisting photographers run a large studio servicing the advertising industry.

   She is assisting in a small business – including advertising and marketing – and acts as a taxi driver for her busy children. Her pleasures include
playing in her vegie garden, cooking, reading and enjoying her family and
friends.

   It is her vision to start a support group for breast cancer patients
with secondaries, as currently most groups only deal with people who have
not had to face and live with a recurrence.

MICHAEL TUNNECLIFFE left a successful practice in Clinical Psychology to become a professional speaker, author and staff development facilitator. His presentations and workshops have been acclaimed across the country and he is a sought-after speaker, especially in the field of emergency services, and health service delivery. Michael can be contacted at: PO Box 106, Palmyra, Western Australia, 6157, or by calling: 61 8 9430 4377.

NOEL WAITE, AO, is Chairman of Waite Consulting Management Group, Director of the Public Transport Corporation and Past President of the Australian Institute of Management.

In 1985 she became Founder President of the Australian Branch of Women Chiefs of Enterprises International (Les Femmes Chefs d'Enterprises Mondiales) and is presently on the World Taskforce for Strategic Planning.

In 1993 Noel was awarded the Officer of the Order of Australia for 'Service to Business and Management, particularly through advancing the development of women in management'.

BRYAN WATERS started his career in 1960 with National Australia Bank, where he held senior executive positions both in Australia and internationally. In 1989 he became the Executive Director of a leading regional bank and in 1992 left banking to establish his own consulting company. In 1993 he joined DBM Australia, where he is the Director for Victoria.

Outside his busy working schedule, Bryan enjoys nothing better than the company of Jude, his wife of fifteen months. He is also an active golfer, tennis player and rower. He has a fourteen-year-old stepson, two grown-up children and one granddaughter living in the United States of America, whom he visits whenever possible.

NOEL WHITTAKER came from a humble farming background to become one of Australia's leading commentators on financial matters. He now reaches over four million people a week through his spot on 7 News, and his columns in major newspapers such as the *Sydney Morning Herald, Brisbane Sunday Mail* and *Perth Sunday Times* and his weekly broadcasts on over fifty radio stations.

He has written five bestselling books and has produced two bestselling audio cassettes and a CD-ROM. He is a speaker of international repute and has addressed audiences of up to 5000 in Australia and overseas. He is also founding director of Whittaker McNaught Pty Ltd, one of Australia's most respected independent financial advisory companies. For his services to the financial planning industry he was named Australian Investment Planner of the Year for 1988.

ROB WILSON is a coach who teaches people how to be successful in the game of life. Drawing on his own hard-learnt lessons, he shows people that focusing on their quality of life will make a difference. He had mapped out his destiny as a professional sportsman, only to have it snatched away in a few moments of violence and pain. Told he would never again take an active part in any sport, Rob thumbed his nose at his doctors and proved them wrong. With new focus, he has rebuilt his life.

JO WILSON is a professional speaker, trainer and success coach. It was during her experience with Cyclone Tracey that Jo realised how easily life can be threatened and that we should all live life to the limit. Jo teaches people to find their direction, to look at their identity and to formulate and achieve their goals. She helps people take their life to a whole new level of meaning and enjoyment.

WILLING TO
HELP OTHERS?

We are dedicated to helping others and hope you are too. If you have, or know of, a story that will inspire and teach others – and you'd like to give to the world through a future version of *There's More to Life than Sex and Money* – please send it to us:

Sue Calwell and Daniel Johnson

c/- Penguin Books Australia Ltd

Adult Publishing Department

PO Box 257

Ringwood VIC 3134

Australia

If the piece is not your own, please provide us with details of the author. We promise you will receive credit.

Thanks very much!

CONTACT
THE AUTHORS
DIRECTLY

ABOUT SUE CALWELL

Sue Calwell has been in the Tourism and Convention industry for over twenty years, until retiring in 1995 from the demands of the corporate life to step back and spend lots of time with her three greatest assets, Georgina, Victoria and Daniel, her children.

She continues her input and commitment to the industry in Australia in her role as Chairman of the World Congress Centre, Melbourne, which also manages the Melbourne Exhibition Centre and the Royal Exhibition Buildings. A new initiative in 1995 saw her Chair the first Melbourne International Flower and Garden Show, a hallmark event for Melbourne, which was an outstanding success. She continues an international involvement with tourism in an advisory capacity to many major events, and both government and private sector consulting, and has recently joined the Board of Tourism Tasmania.

Her greatest challenge of recent times has been taking on the role of full-time mother, cook, housekeeper and taxi driver, which she balances with the love, support and strength of her partner, Alistair.

Sue is available for speaking engagements and you can contact her on: PO Box 652, South Yarra, VIC 3141.

ABOUT DANIEL JOHNSON

Daniel Johnson is one of the best known professional speakers in Australia, New Zealand and south-east Asia. He is known for his enthusiastic approach and his ability to convey the complex issues in an easy to understand and action format. He is regularly a keynote speaker at state, national and international conferences and seminars of all sizes. He is author of several books and hundreds of magazine articles.

Daniel is a devoted family man who practises what he preaches. While writing this book, he has stepped back from his busy schedule to be with his family.

At the time of printing, he is a 'house husband' caring for Eve (eleven years), Jarvis (eight years), Paris (two years), Yasmin (one year), and loving every minute of it. His wife, Kate, is working at a non-profit childcare facility in their local community in Breckenridge, Colorado, USA.

Daniel is available for selected speaking engagements at set times during the year. To contact Daniel for further information about his books, audio tapes, training, or to arrange a speaking engagement, please contact him at:

Daniel Johnson
PO Box 4371
Breckenridge, Co. 80424, USA
Phone/fax: 1 970 547 9886
Email: johnson@vail.net